THE STORY OF

# Sugarloaf

# THE STORY OF
# Sugarloaf

## JOHN CHRISTIE

Cover photograph by Johnna Haskell/ © JohnnaHaskellPhoto.com
Other photographs, unless otherwise noted, courtesy of The Sugarloaf Ski Club,
The Maine Ski Museum, and Sugarloaf/USA

Designed by Chilton Creative
ISBN: 978-0-89272-723-0

Printed in China

5          4          3          2

Down East Books
Camden, Maine
A division of Down East Enterprise
Book orders: 800-685-7962
*www.downeastbooks.com*
Distributed to the trade by National Book Network, Inc.

Library of Congress Cataloging-in-Publication Data

Christie, John.
 The story of Sugarloaf / by John Christie. – 1st ed.
     p. cm.
 Includes index.
 ISBN-13: 978-0-89272-723-0 (trade hardcover : alk. paper)
 1. Sugarloaf USA (Me.) 2. Ski resorts–Maine–History. 3. Skis and skiing–Maine–History. I. Title.
 GV854.5.M2C47 2007
 796.9309741–dc22
                        2007017119

*To my good friend Don Fowler, who, more than anyone, defines the meaning of the word Sugarloafer. His devotion to skiing in general—and Sugarloaf in particular—is legendary. His reminiscences, wit, and occasional wisdom have been invaluable as I've reflected on our shared past at this very special place. Along with all of my skiing buddies, past and present, Don has made returning to my roots at Sugarloaf the most enjoyable odyssey of my life.*

# Contents

# Foreword

If you asked God to build a ski mountain, He would start with a triangle and face it north, with the steepest terrain at the top and gentler slopes at the bottom. He might even throw in some snowfields with above-tree-line skiing and allow for a nice, long intermediate trail from the top so everyone could ski from the summit. This idyllic mountain would also lend itself to one of the most recognizable logos—one that has been seen all over the world. It makes us Sugarloafers so proud when we see the famous Sugarloaf triangle in some of the strangest places.

This is what Amos Winter saw as he drove up Route 27 from Kingfield to Stratton. Not only did he see it, but he had the vision to see it as a ski mountain. The rest is history, and this wonderful book tells you all about Sugarloaf/USA as we know it today.

Who better to write this story than John Christie, the person who worked day and night, summer and winter with Alice and Amos Winter to start the building process of what we have today. If the truth be known, smart money says John has some frozen fingers and toes and scars from black-fly bites to show for his early days as Sugarloaf's general manager.

I have been one of the lucky people to watch the growth of this special place from its beginning, when we had to walk three miles in from Rt. 27 to ski

*Winter's Way and the Access Road, 1952.*

as I did.

Winter's Way, the first trail that Amos and his friends cut. I was part of the team that envisioned a championship golf course—one that would receive the kinds of accolades one only dreams of, and that, more importantly, would put Sugarloaf on the map as a four-season resort. I have also been fortunate to watch Carrabassett Valley Academy grow from a dream to a wonderful place for aspiring kids to show their skiing and snowboarding abilities and still get the kind of education that would allow them to attend the best colleges and grow into caring, responsible citizens.

I have seen the Town of Carrabassett grow from its infancy to become a very willing and helpful partner in all of Sugarloaf's developments.

Equally important in the story of Sugarloaf are the people, who have become the Sugarloaf Family. Because of its relatively remote location, the mountain attracted a certain breed of skier, one who was willing to travel a bit farther to enjoy the natural beauty and power of a big mountain. They have been a very loyal group through all the good and the bad times. Management—starting with Amos, Alice, and John—has always placed a high priority on Sugarloaf being a family area and the people have responded with their unwavering commitment.

This book tells the whole incredible story. I hope you enjoy it as much

—Peter Webber

# Acknowledgments

This book wouldn't have been possible without the patience and tolerance of my wife, Marty, who allowed me the time to explore the archives of Sugarloaf's history, and the freedom to conduct "on-mountain research" (aka, skiing) with all my buddies.

My sons, Josh and Jake, inspired me to return to the sport I loved, and, more important, to the place where it all started for me.

The Locker Room Gang at Sugarloaf is owed a great debt of gratitude for their willingness (and ability) to stroll back in time with me, reawakening powerful memories. And my newly made friends at the Mountain, who arrived after my departure in 1968, have helped fill in the gaps between then and my return in 1995.

Jean Luce and everyone associated with the Ski Museum of Maine have provided immeasurable assistance, not only through their memories, but also their willingness to allow me virtually unlimited access to the Museum's archives.

I am deeply indebted to Paul and Rebecca Crommett for giving me complete access to Dick Crommett's voluminous historical file, as well as the beginning of his history of the Town of Carrabassett Valley, which tragically was never completed due to his untimely passing.

An equal measure of thanks is due to President Bruce Miles and the directors of the Sugarloaf Mountain Ski Club, for opening the Club's files to me

*Riding the original T-Bar, 1955.*

for both research and priceless photographs.

John Diller and his staff at the Mountain have supported me through their enthusiasm for the project and their generosity in providing access not only to the Corporation's archives, but also to the ski lifts, allowing me to immerse myself in the experience of what it means to be a modern-day Sugarloafer.

Dick Bell, great friend through all my years in the ski business and tireless Sugarloaf promoter, produced shortly before his death a written record of the early days, and his family has generously made it available to me.

Heartfelt thanks, and a fond farewell, to Dave Stainton, who, during the past few years, reminded me how magical the sport is—and just how damn much fun it can be.

And, finally, I owe a great debt to what may be one of the world's most unlikely threesomes (the latter posthumously): Neale Sweet, my old friend and publisher of Down East Books, who came to me with this project; Amos Winter, my early mentor in the ski business at Sugarloaf, who taught me that you had to walk before you could run; and Walt Schoenknecht, the fascinating visionary (some say lunatic) who created Mount Snow, had the courage to hire me to run his behemoth in Southern Vermont, and taught me that once you start running, don't stop.

# Prologue

My love affair with Sugarloaf began on a February day in 1954, during my junior year at Camden High School, when Don Worthen and I saw the mountain for the first time. We rode the rope tow up a piece of Winter's Way, climbed the rest of the way up to the edge of the snowfields . . . and I took my first run on a real mountain.

We were spending our Washington's Birthday vacation week at the Exchange Hotel in Farmington, skiing the John Abbott Titcomb Memorial Ski Slope—our first trip away from the Camden Snow Bowl to a real "ski resort." It was a gift from my mother and Don's parents, who sensed that we loved to ski but were beginning to feel confined by the single slope at the Snow Bowl on Ragged Mountain.

During that week, two life-changing events occurred for me: First, I watched in awe as a group of skiing gods and goddesses maneuvered their way effortlessly down the Farmington slopes. I vowed that one day I'd ski half as well as those I jealously attempted to emulate. Little did I know during that fateful February week that I'd not only meet these icons one day, but would also eventually develop lifelong friendships with them: Peter and Norton "Icky" Webber, Brud and Deanie Folger, Jill and Linda Flint, Norton and Suzanne Luce, Norm Twitchell, Tommy Stearns, and a host of other skiing paragons who populated this one special little ski area.

Second, when I rounded "Oh My Gosh" corner on Route 27 north of

*Rounding "Oh My Gosh" Corner, 1957.*

Kingfield and saw, for the first time, the mass of Sugarloaf capped by its glistening snowfields, I somehow sensed that this place would one day become a very important part of my life. I didn't realize then, as a seventeen-year-old high school student, that one day I'd end up racing there during my college years; that I'd spend a spring on the Ski Patrol after returning from postgraduate work in Europe, and stay the following summer to help put in a couple of T-bars; and that eventually I'd end up managing the place.

After leaving in the late 1960s to follow my ski-career star, I finally returned to renew my vows in the mid-'90s, to be ever faithful to my true love: Sugarloaf. My odyssey, and my return, say a lot about this mountain. It inspired me to get into the business in the first place, and years later to rediscover the sport that I'd forgotten I loved so much.

This book is a genuine labor of love. It has given me the opportunity to awaken long-dormant memories of a very special place and time. It has allowed me to explore parts of Sugarloaf's history with which I was either unfamiliar or, I hasten to say, may have just forgotten. It has given me the opportunity to build new friendships with people who have been part of the pageant, and whose roles have made the fabric even more colorful. It has helped me share with my family, none of whom were around during my early years at the Mountain, the details of a very important part of my life. I know that my wife and sons now understand why Sugarloaf has meant—and continues to mean—so much to me.

I'm grateful for the opportunity to offer up my memories to the countless thousands who share my affection for this special place. I pray this book does justice to all those friends of mine, living and dead, who are part of this story. Sugarloaf is, after all, two things: a mountain and a feeling. Both are special and unique. Why they capture us the way they do is tough to explain.

This book is my attempt, however, to do just that.

# A Dream Realized:
## *1945–1961*

**1**

Sugarloaf, as we now know it, began in two places: on the north slope of Bigelow Mountain, and in the head of a storekeeper in Kingfield, Maine, by the name of Amos Winter. It really began in three places, the third being an organization called the Maine Ski Council.

Let me explain. Shortly after the end of World War II, Amos, who owned a general store (actually, the general store) in the sleepy little town of Kingfield, had an idea. He had cut his skiing teeth in the formidable bowl on the east side of Mount Washington known as Tuckerman Ravine, and he began to think he could avoid the long trip to Pinkham Notch if a ski trail of some sort could be cut a little closer to home.

In his backyard loomed Mount Abraham, which he looked at every day from the imposing home he shared with his wife, Alice, on Kingfield's principal height of land, and from their log summer camp a couple of miles away on Tuft's Pond. Farther north up Route 27, toward Stratton and Coburn Gore, were four more 4,000-footers constituting the Longfellow Range, also referred to by some as the Blue Mountains. Amos had tromped those hills, often in the company of his older brother, Erland, a legendary guide and owner of a set of sporting camps called Deer Farm Camps.

Bigelow, the second highest and most massive of those mountains, was of particular interest to Amos. Running some fifteen miles east to west from Little Bigelow to Cranberry Peak, this imposing hulk was the mountain from which Colonel Timothy Bigelow, a member of Benedict Arnold's troop on its march to Quebec in the late fall of 1775, was said to have attempted—unsuccessfully—to see their destination. Interestingly, in March of 1820, when Maine separated from Massachusetts and became a state, Timothy Bigelow was the

*Some of the original Bigelow Boys—years later; l–r: Howard Dunham, Odlin Thompson, Stub Taylor, Howell McClure, Dick French.* **Right:** *An aerial view of Bigelow Mountain across Flagstaff Lake (photo by Mark Warner).*

Speaker of the House of the Massachusetts General Court. Supposedly, the army encamped beyond the great bend of the Dead River and erected a flag at what was later called the town of Flagstaff.

On its broad northerly flank, the potential for a ski trail of nearly 3,000 vertical feet was revealed to Amos as he explored the terrain with Fred Morrison, proprietor of the local drugstore. Accompanying them was an enthusiastic group of young Kingfield schoolboys, including Robert "Stub" Taylor, Odlin Thompson, Howard Dunham, Howell McClure, Dick French, and Mickey Durrell. Together, they ultimately carved out a ski trail.

Their route utilized a section of the Appalachian Trail that started on Avery Peak and descended east toward Little Bigelow, to a point under a promontory known as "The Old Man's Head." Here, the AT intersected with a trail cut by the Civilian Conservation Corps, which headed north toward the old shingle mill on the banks of the Dead River. This so-called Dead River Trail followed the route known today as the Safford Brook Trail.

Starting in the winter of 1945–46, the Bigelow Boys, as they came to be known, enjoyed the deep snows and challenging terrain some twenty miles from Kingfield. But by 1948, the year that marks the real beginning of the Sugarloaf story, the Boys were encountering some problems on Bigelow. Or, better stated, at the base of Bigelow.

## FLAGSTAFF LAKE CREATED

The Central Maine Power Company, recognizing the hydroelectric potential of

the Dead River, had finalized a plan conceived during the 1920s to purchase the land bordering the river north of Bigelow, including the village of Flagstaff, from the Great Northern Paper Company. The plan was to build a dam at Long Falls, not far from the easterly end of Bigelow, and create a massive impoundment to be known as Flagstaff Lake, twenty-six miles long and four to five miles wide at its greatest width. The dam would be built at a total cost of about $6 million. In conjunction with sister dams on the Kennebec, into which the Dead River flowed at The Forks, some twenty miles downriver to the east, this dam would allow the capture and storage of melted winter snows and the subsequent orderly release of water to power-generating stations farther downriver.

As crews began to cut the flowage area, traveling in on a road built to the dam site by the J.L. Hinman Company, a disturbing result was revealed to Amos and the rest of the Bigelow Boys: Their newly cut trail was going to be rendered inaccessible.

During that same year, seventy-five miles southeast of Sugarloaf, in Augusta, the Maine Development Commission—a state government entity appointed by Governor Horace Hildreth—was mulling over various economic-development options for the state. They were aware that ski-area development in Maine's neighboring New England states was contributing a great deal to their economic vitality, including New Hampshire's

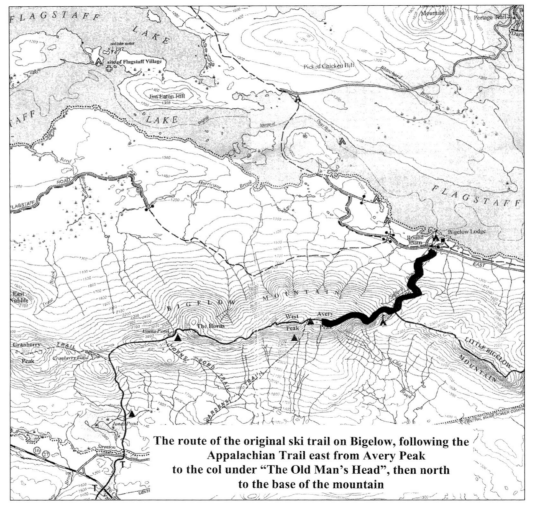

The route of the original ski trail on Bigelow, following the Appalachian Trail east from Avery Peak to the col under "The Old Man's Head", then north to the base of the mountain

public investment in the construction and operation of both Cannon Mountain and Mount Sunapee. Recognizing that skiing might well expand Maine's tourism business not only for the winter season, but also into regions of the state heretofore off the visitors' beaten path, the Commission called a meeting of the handful of existing ski clubs in Maine to start formulating a plan.

This is not to say that ski-area development, of a sort, had not already been well under way in the state. Literally dozens of municipalities had installed rope tows on local slopes, including my personal proving ground, the Camden Snow Bowl. Pleasant Mountain in Bridgton was a flourishing day area for skiers from Portland and surrounding towns, with cable lifts (Maine's first) capable of competing with Cranmore Mountain and other ski areas throughout the Mount Washington Valley.

But to compete with the "big boys," and to spur economic development in more remote areas of the state, a major mountain needed to be identified—and developed.

## THE MAINE SKI COUNCIL IS BORN

The result of that formative session was the creation of the Maine Ski Council, and Robert "Bunny" Bass of Wilton, a name already well known in ski circles for his family company's line of ski boots, was elected the Council's first president.

One of the first orders of business was to appoint from among its membership an Area Development Committee. In the recollected words of Dick Bell of Farmington, Sugarloaf pioneer, promoter, and historian, the Committee's focus would be to "look over all of those mountains in Maine which Maine skiers deemed as developable and determine which of these could be most feasibly turned into a ski area."

Bruce White was named Chairman of the committee, and he was joined by Jim Thorpe, Wes Marco, Bob Henderson, and Horace Chapman, each representing a different existing ski club. Their initial list of potential developments included Saddleback, Sugarloaf, Bigelow, Mount Blue, Farmington, Old Speck, Baldpate, and the Andover Region.

They had heard about Amos' activities on Bigelow, and were aware not only of his access problems, but also of the fact that he had turned his attention to Sugarloaf, the next mountain to the south, and Maine's second highest at more than 4,200 feet. (Although at the time it was thought that Old Speck was higher, a later survey would reveal the discrepancy.)

During 1948, Horace Chapman, Area Development Committee member from the Penobscot Valley Ski Club and owner of the venerable Bangor House, explored the mountain with his son, John (who, incidentally, has the unique distinction of having skied Sugarloaf every year since then).

The only written recollection I've been able to find of skiing that year is by longtime Sugarloafer Phineas Sprague, who was then in his sophomore year at Bowdoin. Sprague was intrigued by Sugarloaf and its most outspoken advocate, Amos Winter. He decided to take a trip north with a few of his college friends to check it out, and called Amos to arrange the trip. Here is an excerpt from his written recollection of that first visit to the mountain in 1948, prepared years later for the Sugarloaf Mountain Ski Club:

*We learned that there was a mountain in Maine, and a man named Amos Winter who knew about it, and that he lived in a town called Kingfield.*

*Amos in the snowfields.*

*On Saturday night before Easter Sunday of that exciting year, three Bowdoin students, and Woody Gar, the captain-elect of the Colby Ski Team, headed for an inspection of this mountain called Sugarloaf. Mr. Winter told us on the phone we could sleep in the ranger cabin that was near a telephone pole with a yellow stripe on it, between Kingfield and Stratton. We finally found it, about midnight, but it was secured by a big padlock. Returning to Kingfield, we slept in the shed at the gravel pit.*

*Before turning in, we put our skis in the snowbank by the side of the road, hoping that the man named Winter might find us in this undesignated meeting place.*

*I had just started a fire to make coffee when a car with its wheels barely touching the ground flew by, and came back. Amos Winter, and his brother Erland, who was a Game Warden, were in the car. Also with him were Robert "Stub" Taylor, Odlin Thompson, and Mickey Durrell.*

*Thoughtful person that Amos was, we hesitated long enough to have some breakfast in Carrabassett, before he led us to the AMC trail that led over the top of Sugarloaf. We carried our skis and climbed in our ski boots. The wind had blown most of the snow off the trail, and after a while we were on top, trying to keep our skis from blowing out of our hands.*

*Stepping off the wind-cleared summit, we were up to our waists in powder snow. With skis on shoulders, it was a good task to find the trail through the thick undergrowth and around the trees. Erland sped down with giant steps on his snowshoes, and as for Amos, after a while he put on his skis with skins (strips of sealskin attached to the bottom of the skis) on. He did pretty well, but he couldn't keep up with Erland.*

*Very clearly, we had found what we were seeking: good terrain with lots of snow. We told the Winters that we'd be back as we departed for Brunswick.*

It wasn't until 1949 that the entire Committee made its first trip to the Carrabassett Valley to get a firsthand look at this mountain they had begun to hear so much about. Accompanied by Amos and his Kingfield protégés, they liked what they saw. They reported back that of all the mountains they had seen, Sugarloaf, in their collective estimation, had the greatest development potential. It combined optimum northerly exposure, the highest annual average snowfall (in excess of 140 inches), and the fewest access issues, with Route 27 running in the valley at its northerly base.

The next year, 1950—just two short years after the creation of the Maine Ski Council—could well be marked as the watershed year in the history of the development of Sugarloaf, for two important events took place.

### THE SUGARLOAF SKI CLUB IS FORMED AND TRAIL WORK BEGINS

First, the Sugarloaf Mountain Ski Club was organized, and second, work began on the initial ski trail. No longer was the arduous work of laying out and cutting a ski trail the exclusive responsibility of a few guys from the surrounding area. Now, willing hands from all over the state were ready to pitch in. And they did.

They recognized that to design a ski trail that would thread its way from the edge of the snowfields down some 1,800 vertical feet to where the concave terrain began to flatten out, about two miles from the main road, would require some professional guidance. Sel Hannah, a nationally known ski-trail designer from Franconia, New Hampshire (and the father, years later, of Olympian Joan Hannah), was asked to lend a hand, and he generously consented.

Before the trail could be laid out and cut, the group had to obtain the permission of the landowner, Great Northern Paper Company. Not only was it granted, but in addition, a twenty-year lease was negotiated for

*Above: Winter's Way. **Below:** Fletcher Brown, Amos, and Stub Taylor rest at Chapman's Corner.*

virtually all of the acreage that would eventually be occupied by the ski-area development. However, this did not include the two miles that needed to be traversed between Route 27 and the lower end of the ski trail. This property was owned by the Merrow family, and, fortunately, they deeded a right-of-way across their land as a generous gift.

The ski trail, to be called Winter's Way, in recognition of the pioneering efforts of its namesake, Amos, was nearly a mile and a quarter in length. It was laid out on the ground by Hannah, and weekend after weekend during the summer of 1950, skiers, friends of skiers, and ski-area aficionados from all over the state gathered on the northerly flank of the mountain to hack out a trail that included, in some areas, pitches in excess of 30 degrees. And at the top of this trail were acres and acres of wide-open snowfields that accumulated snow deposited by the prevailing northwesterly winds during the entire winter, visible into the late spring. Hence, the moniker: Sugarloaf.

Despite the literally thousands of hours of work put in by volunteers, the Ski Club was beginning to incur some expenses associated with the initial stages of ski-area development. The Club obtained its financial support in two ways. According to the minutes taken by Scott Scully (a skier and Portland attorney for the Maine Central Railroad) at a formative meeting of the Club: "At the end of the meeting, the Treasurer reported a balance of $80 in the treasury as a result of a spontaneous digging into pockets on the part of a group of those present."

This generosity was one of the revenue streams, which also included donations and in-kind contributions, such as the use of a bulldozer for access-road construction by the Dead River Company, a large landowner in the area.

The other source of financial support was the sale of annual memberships in the Sugarloaf Mountain Ski Club, at $10 a member.

The twelve folks who attended the first Ski Club meeting at the Augusta House constitute a virtual Who's Who of luminaries, whose names would become inextricably connected with Maine skiing in general, and Sugarloaf in particular: George Albert, Fletcher Brown, Horace Chapman, John and Peg Clark, Bill Hatch, Wes Marco, Scott Scully, Phin Sprague, "Stub" Taylor, Odlin Thompson, and, of course, Amos Winter. By the winter of 1950–51, this nucleus of interested Mainers felt their dream might be realized. It was a good snow year, and marked what would become a Sugarloaf tradition: skiing the mountain well into May. Enthusiastic skiers braved the primitive two-mile access road, hiked up to the snowfields, often using skins on the bottoms of their hickories, and, on a good day, got in two top-to-bottom runs on the longest and most challenging trail in Maine.

Many of them, like Horace Chapman, would pack sleeping bags and camp out just below the timberline so they could get in their initial run at first light, which occasionally allowed them to get in three full runs before late afternoon.

The best—and, in fact, only known—written record in the archives of skiing during that inaugural season appeared in *Appalachia,* the journal of the Appalachian Mountain Club. It was written by Andrew A. Titcomb, a Farmington native then living in Perkinsville, Vermont. An architect, Andrew had developed his skiing skills while an undergraduate at Dartmouth, and by 1951 had skied most of the then-operating ski areas in the East. His bylined story was entitled SKIING MAINE'S UNKNOWN SNOWFIELDS, and it gives us a graphic sense of what Sugarloaf was like in 1951.

*Snowfields above timberline in Maine? On Katahdin, you may say, but that's almost inaccessible in wintertime. No, this is much nearer at hand, open, smooth snowfields, long and steep, that you can ski with safety almost anytime, unlike the higher mountains, with snow lasting into May—and there you have the Blue Mountains of Western Maine, of which 4,237-foot Sugarloaf Mountain is the queen, Maine's second-highest mountain.*

*A 4,000-foot peak does not sound high enough to fulfill these conditions, and that is perhaps why this superb ski area has remained without a track on it all these years. But its location is the secret. Within sight of the Rangeley Lakes and surrounded by no less than five other distinct 4,000-foot giants, with their valley floors all above 1,000 feet above the sea, it may well prove the most reliable snow district in the East. And so it proved this year, not merely in early March, but April 26 and 27, 1951, when I found five to fifteen feet of snow on top and three feet on the new ski trail over halfway down, and this was a poor snow year.*

*A two-year-old hope to ski Sugarloaf was fulfilled on April 25. I called Amos Winter of Kingfield, Maine, perennial skier, general store*

*The pioneers on the Access Road, 1950; l–r: Amos, Bob Scott, Taino Maki, "Bunny" Bass, Richard Luce, Horace Chapman, Jim Flint, George Cary, George Mendall.*

owner, and the "father" of this mountain. In Farmington, 30 miles to the south, it was warm, the spring flowers were coming out, and people were oiling up the old lawn mower. "I suppose I'm too late again to ski Sugarloaf this year?" I asked Amos over the party line.

"Too late, my eye!" he replied. "I can see the snowfields out my store window, and they're deeper and whiter than ever."

That very afternoon, with ski and pack, tent and sleeping bag, I was headed north to fulfill a dream started by my brother years before, when we climbed the mountain in summer up the Appalachian Trail, and revived two years ago, when at the top of the left gully in Tuckerman Ravine, Amos had told me of the newly formed Sugarloaf Mountain Ski Club and of their plans to cut a ski trail down from the snowfields on the north face.

By the time I checked in at Winter's store, a cold northwest wind had hit Kingfield with a sprinkle of rain, but the snow reports were confirmed, though the summits of Mount Abraham and Sugarloaf were now under a scud of fast-moving somber clouds. On the way to Stratton the road borders the rushing Carrabassett River, which looked to be a good canoeing height. The country rapidly gets wilder and more rugged up this valley, as the road twists between the mountains and the houses become fewer. In half an hour I saw the Sugarloaf Ski Club sign on the left, just below deserted Bigelow Village.

After the car was parked, there came the start of a long trip in. It was 4 o'clock now, and the first glimpse of a winding white streak of a ski trail could be seen dipping down out of the clouds between the dark spruces. After a rough and very wet walk of some two miles on the level, including crossing several swollen brooks, with not the least sign of snow, there appeared, quite suddenly, rising up across the bank of a rushing stream, the ski trail; and there the snow began, at about 1,700 feet.

From here on I climbed on skis with sealskins—a rest for weary shoulders—up the trail, which wound up through the hardwoods, over snow still drenched from the rain of the previous night. By 6 o'clock, some two hours up, I decided to call it a day, and make camp before darkness caught me.

The ski trail gleamed faintly white as it sloped off to the north. The clouds had been swept away by the sweep of the northwest winds and the cold stars glittered down above the forest. From this vantage point, 2,000 feet up on Sugarloaf, the clear outline of the mountains to the north could be seen, but there was the light of no single habitation in the wilderness valley below.

The next morning, breakfast was eaten in the warmth of the sun rising over Burnt Hill, and then I made an 8:00 A.M. start for the summit, with a light lunch packed this time.

At 3,000 feet I was nearly through the spruces, the fine wide trail reminding me of the upper part of the "Wildcat." Repeated thrusts of a ski pole, handle down, into the snow right up to the ring, failed to reach the bottom—long poles at that. The heat of the sun had thawed the frozen granules of spring snow by now so that walking was easy, and as I rounded a final bend, I saw a wide chute opening directly to the dazzling snowfield above, a breathtaking first glimpse of the open cone of the summit. As the trees ended, the open slopes climbed toward the blue sky at an angle of 40 degrees, and it was a matter of dig and kick your toes in to climb that last thousand feet. Here and there the tops of subalpine birch and hackmatack showed their tops through the snow, covered with clear frost feathers of ice built up on the northwest side of each branch. The depth of the snow cover here must have been a solid blanket of five to fifteen feet deep, drifted in on the north side of this mountain.

Up and up I went, leaving a trail of footsteps behind in the perfect spring snow. The slope gradually tilted back to a steady 30 degrees nearer the summit. Finally came the last scramble over some dark weathered rocks and lichen to the topmost cairn. My watch read 10:15 as I rested my skis against the rocks and looked around in the crystal-clear morning air.

Now for the first run down! A check of bindings—tighten those laces, zip those pockets, sealskins in the pack. Boy, this **is** steep!—and we're off.

You don't have to pick your way, it's all open, smooth spring snow, ever steepening as it drops away to timberline a thousand feet below. The skiing you wait all year for, great sweeping turns, the incredible acceleration at the instant your tips point straight down,

*and yet snow so smooth and even you feel you could shut your eyes and ski, as in a dream. But a thousand feet does not take long at this rate, and soon you are at the edge of the trees, breathless after the flight down. This is good—so up to the summit again, exploring dif-*

*the same smooth breathless drop, then through some scrub, 'til there below lay the funnel through the trees, with the trail beyond. The snow is warmer and heavier now, as you catch your breath, wipe your eyes, and eat a last bar of chocolate, while you take a final gaze up that never-to-be-forgotten snowfield, and then a plunge down into the trail, with a view at every turn. In a matter of minutes the hardwoods appear, and shortly thereafter, a tired christy brings you to a stop at camp. You take a rest on the bough bed before breaking camp, and then start the final descent through slushy snow, now turned pink by the after-noon sun, to the brook crossing at the foot of the ski trail prop-er.*

**Left:** *Press coverage of the Sugarloaf Schuss.* **Right:** *Young Brud Folger racing down Winter's Way.*

*ferent routes and eating frost feathers as you go. It was time for lunch now in the lee of the cairn, and a look at the logbook rolled up in the bronze A.T.C. cylinder. Only 16 names were recorded this first winter of skiing on the mountain, but note the marker had been buried in frost feathers much of the time.*

*I took a last look around at the great wilderness stretching for miles upon miles all around, and then started the run down again, to the left this time on the western part of the snowfields. There was*

*Here is a mountain, less than 185 miles from the heart of Boston, with open snow-fields above timberline and snow conditions seldom equaled in the East, that was never skied until this last win-ter of 1950–51! For thrills and scenery, real open skiing and a great ski trail, put Sugarloaf Mountain on your books for that long weekend this winter.*

The summer of 1951 was a busy one on the mountain, as Amos and his crew undertook trail widening and grooming, as well as rock picking. The latter became an annual tradition during all the summers prior to the installation of snowmaking equipment, as crews would try to remove all the rocks pushed up to the surface each year by the winter frost. The rocks would be picked and tossed off into the woods. My own earliest memories of working on the mountain are punctuated by what seemed like interminable hours picking rocks and swallowing blackflies in May and June!

And during that summer, in a tradition that has now become endemic to the ski industry, debt was incurred. Gravel was needed for the access road to ensure its dependable use, and Jim Flint, president of Peoples National Bank of Farmington, stepped up to the plate and provided a loan to the Club (secured, of course, by the personal signatures of the directors) for the much-needed improvements.

Although access to the base of Winter's Way was improved, the 1951-52 ski season still saw skiers enduring the arduous climb to avail themselves of the skiing.

It was another good year for snow, and the *Portland Press Herald* reported, "In April, there were five to fifteen feet of hard-packed corn snow near the summit." This exceptional accumulation was the result of two factors. First, the prevailing westerly winds would blow snow from the top of the mountain over the summit onto the easterly side, much like the phenomenon that results in the huge annual depths in Tuckerman Ravine on Mount Washington. And second, history shows that, on average, it snowed more during the 1950s than in more recent years.

Also, that year, on April 6, Wes Marco chaired the committee that launched the inaugural Sugarloaf Schuss, won by Ted Hawkes of the Down East Ski Club in Portland. The race was held to demonstrate to the world the racing potential of the Mountain, to publicize the completion of the first trail, and to showcase the area's abundant April snow. In addition to winner Hawkes, forty-six other men and women competed. Notable participants included Dave Farrell, Bob Irish, Jack Beattie, Henry Poirier, Brud Folger, Aurele Legere, Peter and Icky (who was twelve at the time) Webber, and Stubb Taylor. Edith Curtis, who won the women's event, was joined by, among

*Left: Sugarloaf, 1952.* **Upper right:** *The original ski club building.* **Lower right:** *The mountain seen from "Oh My Gosh" Corner, 1952.*

others, Erland Winter's daughter, Amanda, who was encouraged to enter by her uncle, Amos.

Esther Perne's written record of that first race, entitled "The Birth of Sugarloaf Ski Racing," appeared in the 50th Anniversary Magazine of the Sugarloaf Mountain Ski Club in the year 2000. Here is an excerpt:

*Preparations for that first race, by today's standards, were rudimentary. Sandwiches were prepared for each racer to carry (along with their bulky equipment) on the two-hour hike to the summit. Coffee was hauled up by volunteers, also on foot. A tractor with a sledge was procured to transport equipment from Route 27. And, a few poles and borrowed flags were collected for the course. As they climbed the course and came near the top of the snowfields, racer Bob Irish recalls, "Course Setter Wes Marco had run out of bamboo poles. Being an ingenious 'Mainer,' he proceeded to cut down the tops of some spruce trees which he trimmed as they went along, and set the last several gates, including a flush, with three-inch-diameter sticks."*

*As Sugarloaf's ski racing program developed, it was the Schuss that became legend. In the mid-sixties it was one of the biggest races of the year, attracting up to 400 entrants.*

During the summer of 1952, the trail was further groomed, and the initial base lodge—a hut, actually—was constructed at about the 2,200-foot level at the bottom of Winter's Way, under the direction of Fred Morrison, chairman of the newly formed Hut Committee.

It was during this summer that Rand Stowell of Dixfield would begin his long-term involvement with Sugarloaf. It was Rand who had first introduced Joe Dodge, legendary skier and his classmate at Dartmouth, to the Mountain, convincing him to do some terrain assessment and trail layout. In fact, Rand's widow, Phoebe, shared with me a wonderful story that says a lot about Rand, and even more about the attitude of many involved in the early development of Sugarloaf.

After a visit to Sugarloaf, Joe stopped to have dinner in Dixfield on his way home to Franconia with Rand, Phoebe, and their three young sons. When Rand asked him for his assessment of the mountain, Joe is reported to have said, "It'll make a fabulous ski area, but you'll never get people to come that far, all

*Climbing Winter's Way*

the way from Boston." To which Rand is said to have replied, "Good; that's just the way we want it!" Therein is manifested some of the early tension between those (like the Development Commission and Bill Hatch of the Maine Publicity Bureau) who saw the economic potential of such a development, and those whose sole interest was in developing a ski area close to home for Maine skiers. History has shown us dramatically that these objectives were not mutually exclusive, but were, in fact, compatible, and collectively responsible for the ultimate success of Sugarloaf.

Rand demonstrated his enthusiasm for the project that summer with the loan of a bulldozer from his Timberlands Corporation, augmented with another machine donated by Forster Mfg. Co., Inc. in Wilton.

Although every skier who had climbed the Mountain to ski Winter's Way had thought and talked about how great it would be to have a lift to take them at least partway up the trail, it was nothing but a pipe dream and speculative chatter until the summer of 1952, when the talk not only grew louder, but also began to result in some concrete action.

The Ski Club knew that the biggest hurdle to the installation of a lift was the financial one, because the Club had virtually no money. What resources they had were spent on trail grooming, improving the access road, and building the warming hut. Additionally, rescue toboggans had been purchased and sheltered in strategically placed caches, a transaction that further depleted the treasury.

At an executive committee meeting of the Ski Club in December 1952, secretary George Cary noted that "the type, length, location or locations of up-ski devices were discussed . . . everyone thought one would be nice."

The 1952–53 ski season saw a continuation of dependable snow, and the Sugarloaf Schuss was run in the spring with nearly ideal conditions. The access road held up well during the thaw, and the warming hut fulfilled its purpose. More and more people were discovering how wonderful it was to ski this behemoth of a mountain, difficult as it was to climb.

The Ski Club members were realizing that the next step—installation of a lift, or lifts—would far exceed the potential financial capacity of their all-volunteer organization, and discussions were ongoing about where those resources might be found. Was there an individual (or a group) willing to risk investing the money that was needed to move the development forward?

These deliberations continued into the summer of 1953, during which time there was a flurry of activity. A shelter was constructed just below the timberline at a point very close to what was to become, in 1961, the location of the upper terminal of the mountain's fifth T-bar, and, after that, the upper terminal for the King Pine Chair.

### THE ROPE TOW

Even more important, the first tow, modest as it was, was installed on the lowest section of Winter's Way in 1953. Seven hundred feet long, and powered by a 10-horsepower gasoline engine, this rope tow allowed accomplished skiers to get a short assist on their ascent to the top. Beginners could use it to learn some rudimentary turns on easy terrain on the gentler, lower part of the mountain.

Stub Taylor ran the lift (in addition to caring for any injured skiers) on the weekends, and Sugarloaf began to generate its initial lift income by charging skiers who were not members of the Club a fee to use the tow: $1.00 per day for adults, and 50 cents for juniors (children age 12 and under.)

*Sugarloaf Schuss awards ceremony.*

The Club made sure that an interested and supportive media was kept informed of its activities, and the *Portland Press Herald,* in particular, was both receptive to news and generous in its coverage of developments at Sugarloaf. Robert "Bunny" Bass, the Club's president, was particularly adept at getting, and keeping, the media's attention, as indicated in a story that ran in the *Press Herald* in November of 1953:

*Robert N. Bass says that a chairlift to the top of the Mountain, plus modern accommodations in the vicinity, would attract not only skiers from all over the East, but visitors in all other seasons who would use the lift to see the magnificent view from the summit. These, however, would call for the expenditure of a lot of money, far more than the Club will ever have. However, if private capital wishes to invest in this venture, the Club will give all those involved all the cooperation possible.*

And so began the 1953–54 ski season, with the rope tow providing great assistance to "leg-weary veterans of skin-encumbered hikes," as described by Dick Bell in his recollections of Sugarloaf's earliest days. Hundreds of beginning skiers were able to enjoy countless runs on the relatively easy terrain accessed by the lift, and people who had only read about the mountain were now able to experience it firsthand.

Snow was once again plentiful, and the Sugarloaf Schuss, now a staple on the United States Eastern Amateur Ski Association's calendar of important, "do not miss" races, was run as a giant slalom and was won by Les Streeter, a sophomore at Middlebury College. Les was distinguished in my mind for two additional reasons: I knew and revered Les when he was the freshman roommate of my older brother, Mick, at Middlebury, and I watched him later with great pride as a key member of the 1956 U.S. Olympic Team.

The search continued for the financial help that would allow the Club to realize its dream of developing the Mountain to its full potential—accelerated, principally, under the prodding of President Bass and director Scott Scully.

During the fall of 1954, when those of us living on the coast were experiencing the wrath of hurricanes Carol and Edna, the Mountain experienced only minor washouts of the access road. Amos and his summer crew of volunteers widened Winter's Way, both in the lower reaches serviced by the rope tow, and at the point where skiers dropped into the trail from the snowfields.

By the 1954–55 ski season, a scant four years after the first flickering flame of an idea was ignited, Sugarloaf had a facility with a one-

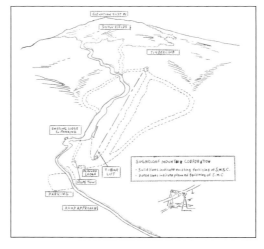

***Top:*** *Sugarloaf Ski Club annual meeting at the expanded clubhouse.* ***Above left:*** *An impromptu gathering some early board members; back row l–r: Richard Luce, Dick Bell, "Bunny" Bass, George Cary; front row l–r: Bob Scott, Amos Winter, George Mendall*

and-a-half-mile trail, a two-mile access road, a large parking lot, a warming cabin at the foot of the trail, a rope tow, first-aid equipment (with people trained to use it), and two rescue toboggans.

Even more important, there was a palpable sense that this place could really become something—if only the money could be found to make it happen.

### THE SUGARLOAF MOUNTAIN CORPORATION

Then, on March 24, 1955, at the Worcester House in downtown Hallowell, a group of energetic visionaries formed the Sugarloaf Mountain Corporation. Elected as its first officers were Bunny Bass, president; Richard Luce, owner of the Farmington Oil Company, vice president; Dick Bell, owner of the Currier Insurance Agency in Farmington, secretary and clerk; and Jim Flint, president of Peoples National Bank of Farmington, treasurer. Amos Winter was formally named executive manager, and a thirteen-member board was elected.

One hundred thousand dollars' worth of common stock was authorized and issued at $10 par. The Sugarloaf Ski Club received a thousand shares in compensation for all of the existing facilities—not a bad deal for the investors, since the Club had previously borrowed $10,000 just to improve the access road!

The group of dedicated, uncompensated directors met frequently in

Hallowell, Wilton, Farmington, Sugarloaf, and at numerous other locations where the group, or parts of it, could easily convene. And as active as this group was, Amos and his crew were even busier on the Mountain.

After lengthy discussion, the consideration of a range of options, countless hours of research, and tough bargaining by a parsimonious and persistent President Bass, a contract was signed with the E. G. Constam Company of Denver to buy a 3,750-foot T-bar lift for $42,500. The Corporation archives reveal that the lift was originally quoted at about $50,000, but Bass was able to skillfully negotiate a substantially lower price.

### THE FIRST T-BAR

The lift, ascending about 900 vertical feet from a new warming hut to be built during the summer, and capable of loading some 800 skiers per hour, was installed under the direction of the imaginative and indomitable Win Robbins and his Robbins Engineering Company of Westbrook. Robbins was named the first lift inspector for Maine's Passenger Tramway Safety Board, and served as my mentor at both Sugarloaf and Saddleback.

The Narrow Gauge trail was laid out and cut on the skiers' left, looking down the mountain from the top of the new lift, and the warming hut—actually a genuine base lodge—was built, complete with a food-service operation leased to Leo and Margaret Scribner from Stratton. This remarkable couple, and their extended family and staff from the Stratton-Eustis area, continued to provide food service for years to come, on a larger and larger scale, even including an operation on the second floor of the upper terminal of the gondola, to be installed years later.

During the 1955–56 ski season, the infant Sugarloaf Mountain Corporation realized a net operating profit, after taxes, of $2,798.68, on operating revenues of slightly more than $20,000. Heady stuff for a brand-new business, and perhaps the highest return-on-investment the Corporation would ever attain. The directors, characteristically, voted to plow the money back into the area and add it to the surplus available for future development projects. Much

*President "Bunny" Bass signs the contract for the first T-Bar as treasurer Jim Flint looks on—and holds his breath.*

## Fresh Snowfall Highlights Sugarloaf Lift Dedication

### By PAT HARTY

KINGFIELD, Me., Jan. 29—Robert Bass, president of the Sugarloaf Mountain ski area, 15 miles east on route 27 from here, dedicated its 3860-foot T bar lift to the youth of New England in simple ceremonies this afternoon. The ceremony over, a record crowd of over 2000 got back to skiing on 2 to 6 inches of fresh snow.

Speaker of the House of Representatives, Willis Trafton of Auburn, Me., the Republican candidate for governor, was principal speaker and interrupted skiing with his four children just one minute and 17 seconds.

Roger Peabody, executive secretary of the Eastern Ski Association, who has skied here many times, spoke for the skiers and encouraged Maine. Now that it has wet its feet in the ski business to "keep up the good work until this great mountain area hereabouts is covered with lifts.

Skiing was good here today after an early morning snowfall that covered the icy spots of yesterday and hundreds used the new T bar.

Today was certainly children's day here with hundreds of families bringing the youngsters for a big day on the new runs.

The bottom of the T bar lift is 1800 feet above sea level. From Kingfield at 500 feet it is a constant rise over the 15-mile brand new highway. Much of which is under construction still. . . . To get here follow the new super highway as far as Auburn. Take Route 4 to Farmington and then follow Route 27 right to the 2-mile access road to the lift. . . .

This road is quite a story. It cost the ski club $10,000 in cash plus another $10,000 in donated bulldozer and truck time that members cajoled from local con-tractors. It, like the lift, is all paid for. . . .

Harry Pollard, Lowell skier, was here today after a night drive from Waterville Valley in New Hampshire. . . . Sumny Sunderland, the Lawrence banker, skied here today after devoting the morning to picking himself a site for a cottage at the junction of Route 27 and the access road. . . .

Oliver Chesaux, French teacher at the University of Maine, who taught skiing for Paul Valeer at Franconia during the Christmas week, heads the ski school here and had some good classes today.

Robert "Stub" Taylor of Kingfield is head of the ski patrol and is here seven days a week. He is assisted by a volunteer patrol. If he ever needs help all he has to do is put out a call for Dr. Stanley Covert of Kingfield who skis here every spare minute.

Amos Winter, area manager, says they will cut the two long runs that parralled the lift wider so they will compare with the north and south slopes at North Conway. Now they are about half that width.

Wesley Marco of Bath, who is the ski coach of the Farmington High School ski team, state champ, set a giant slalom on the right hand slope today for a fun race for some of the better skiers on the mountain.

Alex Bright and Jimmy Madden of Boston, with Lowell Thomas of radio fame are all stockholders in the mountain.

Clarence Wyman, electrical appliance manufacturer from Brockton, is one of the directors of the mountain properties and skied here over the week-end.

of the board's confidence, which spurred them on to aggressively continue development of the area, came from the enthusiastic response of skiers and other interested investors who rapidly subscribed to the initial offering. How were those original shares so effectively merchandised? In about every way imaginable! Every director carried subscriptions around in their pockets, and never missed an opportunity to sell a share or two. No skier escaped Amos and his wife Alice when they stepped up to buy a lift ticket. Many people who came up to the mountain for a day of skiing left as owners.

I have an old friend, a mere youth in the summer of 1955, who recalls sitting on the porch of a camp on Clearwater Lake near Farmington one evening, when a canoe pulled up to the dock, occupied by Bunny Bass and Dick Bell. They had been paddling around the lake, stopping at the camps of friends and strangers alike, trying to interest the occupants in investing in this thing called Sugarloaf. My friend Neale Sweet remarked years later that this method of selling stock gave a whole new meaning to the phrase "floating a stock offering."

During the 1955–56 season, the Mountain opened its first Ski School (weekends only) under the direction of accomplished skier and instructor Olivia "Ollie" Cheseaux, a native Swiss and a student at the University of Maine at Orono.

In February, an Oliver snow-packer tractor became Sugarloaf's first major piece of grooming equipment. Its arrival didn't mark the end of the traditional technique of sidestepping, foot-packing slope preparation, however, which would continue for years on terrain inaccessible to grooming machinery.

Years later someone remarked to me that he could remember when Amos would give a skier a lift ticket in exchange for a half-day of foot-packing,

**Left:** *Winter's Way.* **Right:** *Lined up for the T-Bar*

to which I responded, "I can remember when Amos wouldn't even **sell** someone a ticket until they'd put in some foot-packing time!"

Here's a good place for what might be my favorite recollection about Amos's storied Yankee frugality, and his sense that **anyone** who had the privilege of skiing Sugarloaf should pay the going price, regardless of who they were. I was standing with him in the ticket office on a spring day in 1966, after the Gondola had begun operation, when who should appear at the window but Mike Strauss, the ski writer for *The New York Times.*

Strauss could make or break the reputation of a ski area with a few lines in his column, read by millions.

Strauss stepped up to the window, stuck his hand through the opening to shake Amos's hand, and said, "Good morning. I'm Mike Strauss from *The New York Times.*" At this point, I'm sure he expected his complimentary press pass to be humbly tendered. He hadn't reckoned on Amos, however, who, without blinking an eye, responded, "I'm Amos Winter from Kingfield....That'll be ten dollars."

The 1955–56 ski season was another great year for snow, and the lifts were able to run through Sunday, May 6.

## THE SECOND T-BAR

The summer of 1956 saw a flurry of activity on the Mountain as the next development phase took place. It was all captured in a letter from the Corporation, sent out to ski enthusiasts far and wide:

*Sugarloaf beckons you to come to its slopes this coming winter, and there enjoy skiing at its best from EARLY DECEMBER TILL LATE MAY, which is no idle fantasy.*

*The 1955–56 ski season at SUGARLOAF was so successful that the Directors unanimously voted to increase the facilities for your skiing pleasure by installing the following:*

▲ *An additional 2,600-ft. Constam T-bar in tandem with an existing lift to carry skiers well up into the snowfields—a distance of 6,240 feet from the base area.*

▲ *The Lodge has now been enlarged to a building 110 feet*

*long, where skiers may rest and watch activities on the various trails, from the eight picture windows. The Lodge also includes a large and modern commissary where the finest home-cooked foods are served.*

▲ *You will be delighted with the modern restroom facilities. Running hot and cold water is on tap from the Corporation's own artesian well drilled deep into the mountain.*

▲ *For those of you who should fall by the hillside (we hope you don't), peace and comfort will be derived in the newly equipped first-aid room. Here splints of all kinds are available, and prompt attention will be given in the event of mishap.*

▲ *For equipment, just visit us—that is all we ask. If, when you see the slope, you feel that inner urge to feel the tingle of crisp, clean, invigorating racing as you skim down our inviting trails, then let your fancy take over and visit HARVEY'S SKI SHOP—one of the most completely outfitted shops of this nature in the East, where all types of ski equipment may be purchased or rented.*

▲ *After satisfying your soul with the panoramic view from atop SUGARLOAF, with the Canadian Mountains in the north, the famous Bigelow Range to the east, while below you the country is pockmarked by scattering lakes and rolling hills, several ways are open to you for your descent. By traversing Sugarloaf's snowfields to*

**Above:** *Suzanne Luce and Jill Flint ride the T-Bar.* **Below:** *"Bunny" Bass looks on as Ann Bell cuts the ribbon, while Louise Gulick and Linda Flint wait to be the first passengers up the new lift.*

the south, you have here the only true alpine skiing in the snowfields above timberline in the East. Here you encounter the famous chute at the head of "Winter's Way." This is the original Sugarloaf trail which is known to so many skiers throughout the East; the upper half of which offers a real challenge to the expert and intermediate skier, while the lower half presents a paradise for the intermediate and novice. Truly a mile and three-quarters of unforgettable experience.

▲ The "Sluice" and upper half of "Narrow Gauge" should only be traversed by the experts. Here one drops a thousand feet over 35-degree trails to the halfway station, in the first half-mile. The "Sluice" then enters "Winter's Way" at the spring and thence continues approximately a mile, giving an opportunity to regain one's composure from this breathtaking descent through the "Sluice" to the Lodge.

▲ The "Upper Half of Narrow Gauge" offers equal challenges to the expert, with a corresponding vertical, winding descent to the halfway terminal. Then, over one of the widest and best-groomed mountain slopes, one drops another 900 feet to the Lodge, in three-quarters of a mile.

▲ The "Tote Road," a completely new two-and-one-half-mile trail, starting at the upper terminal near the snowfields, meanders lazily along the north ridge, parallel to the famous "Appalachian Trail," for a distance of three-quarters of a mile, where it then turns to the east, drops rapidly, and then sweeps into another gradual slope which swings gently down through heavy timber for nearly a mile and a half to the Lodge.

▲ SKI PATROL: Full-time and volunteer Ski Patrolmen will be in attendance at all times and are on constant alert for accidents on the trails. These patrolmen may be alerted over a communication system that extends from the Lodge to key points on all trails.

▲ SUGARLOAF MOUNTAIN SKI SCHOOL will be in daily operation after December 15th, under the direction of "Bill" Briggs. Bill comes to us highly recommended as a certified instructor

**Above:** Sugarloaf, 1955. **Below:** The base lodge, phase one.

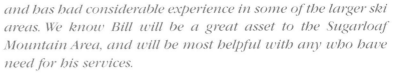

*and has had considerable experience in some of the larger ski areas. We know Bill will be a great asset to the Sugarloaf Mountain Area, and will be most helpful with any who have need for his services.*

▲ *Accommodations in motels, hotels, and private homes in adjacent towns are available.*

*December 15th is the official opening date, although if conditions permit, the lifts may be in operation before that time.*

There's little to add to the above picture of what Sugarloaf had to offer for the 1956–57 ski season, except for a couple of additions and clarifications. First, the Harvey of Harvey's Ski Shop was the unforgettable Harvey Boynton, whose name is as synonymous with the history of the Mountain as anyone who ever lived. Those of us who got to know this unusual man are truly blessed. May he rest in peace!

The first Tucker Sno-Cat (complete with roller) was added to the grooming fleet, and a garage was built to house it, along with the Mountain's other rolling stock. The new lift would have a capacity of some 400 passengers per hour.

The old outhouse, displaced by inside plumbing, was not abandoned. Sugarloaf regular John Parker invented the first ski locker at Sugarloaf by

**Upper and lower left**: *The expanded base lodge takes shape.* **Upper and lower right:** *Sugarloaf seen from the Access Road.*

picking up a padlock and hasp at Jordan Lumber in Kingfield, allowing his family to safely store their gear under lock and key in the unused outhouse, right there on the Mountain. Little did he know that such lockers would become a profit center in later years for Harvey Boynton, and later, the Mountain Corporation (but not in abandoned outhouses!).

Finally, Brooks Dodge of Dartmouth and U.S. Olympic Team fame—and the son of Joe Dodge—laid out the Tote Road, for which generations of Sugarloaf skiers will be eternally grateful. In the late 1970s I had the privilege of getting to know Brookie and working with him when we sat together on the Wildcat board of directors. I've always thought of him as representing the best of what the world of skiing has to offer.

The list of available accommodations for skiers included the twenty bunk beds in the Ski Club building, at $1.00 for members and $1.50 for nonmembers (bring your own sleeping bag); the Arnold Trail Hotel in Stratton at $6.00; a bed at Blanche Goodwin's in Kingfield for $2.50; and Record's Camps (later Tague's) in Carrabassett ($2.50 with linen, $2.00 with sleeping bag). In total, more than 300 beds were available from Eustis to Kingfield for overnight visitors, including the venerable Hotel Herbert in Kingfield, which had reopened under new owner Alvin Westman after having been closed for twenty-seven years.

The 1956–57 ski season, which started on December 28, proved to be auspicious in a most unfortunate way. For the first time since Sugarloaf had opened, a snow drought hit the entire Northeast. It adversely affected skiing conditions and, of course, the amount of visitors to the Mountain. Despite the lack of snow, with only 124 inches recorded for the season (in contrast to the normal 150 inches or more), income derived from the sale of lift tickets increased from about $20,000 during the 1955–56 season to nearly $32,000—an encouraging sign. And an additional $1,400 was realized from equipment rentals. That said, the operation still

*Left:* Rounding "Oh My Gosh" Corner, 1957. ***Right:*** Sugarloaf mounts its first advertising campaign.

sustained a net loss of $9,518.58, almost all of which was attributable to an increase in depreciation of about that amount due to recently made capital investments.

Nonetheless, expansion continued during the summer of 1957. Werner Rothbacher, a certified Austrian ski instructor, was hired to head the Ski School. Bob Verrier and Vic Schlich of AdVentures, Inc., a Portland advertising agency, were chosen to handle marketing and publicity. Extensive grooming was undertaken on the trails, safety devices were installed on the lifts, additional ski patrol equipment was purchased, and the seemingly interminable work on the access road continued.

In August, the Corporation authorized and offered to the public 8,000 additional shares of stock at $10 per share, with the $80,000 proceeds allocated to help pay for improvements already made: the 2,600-foot T-bar, $57,000; new trails, $15,000; lodge addition, water system, piping and plumbing, $11,000; and equipment, $4,700.

Later in the fall, the Corporation sent a notice to shareholders of record and other interested parties, stating, in part:

*The Company has now been in operation two operating years, offering skiers two Constam T-bar lifts in tandem—the lower 3,640 feet in length with a vertical rise of 870 feet and the upper 2,600 feet with a vertical rise of 960 feet. The combined lifts service two expert (upper) to intermediate (lower) trails paralleling the lifts on either side, and a long intermediate-novice trail approximately two and one-half miles long. All trails serviced by the lower lift have been graded and seeded and the trails on the upper areas of the mountain will be groomed as time and finances allow during this summer.*

**Above:** *The original base lodge and the first lift-line maze.* **Below:** *Leo Scribner rings up a sale.*

*The Company lodge was enlarged almost double in space during the summer of 1956, making room for an expanded commissary, manager's office, ski shop, and modern restrooms. Heat and running water were provided, The Company purchased a Sno-Cat with rollers for rolling the ski trails and for use in its First-Aid Service. A small tractor has also been of great value.*

*Operations during the season just completed were hampered in no small way by the lack of heavy snowfalls. This condition prevailed throughout all Eastern ski areas. As a result, the Company did not feel it safe to run the new or upper lift for the skiing public. Operating income, though 63 percent greater than in 1955–56, was limited due mainly to this factor. Access trails from unloading points on the upper lift are being cut across to the upper trails to allow the public to use the upper lift prior to the time when the snowfield areas will be skiable this coming season.*

*Financially, the Company was able to use bank credit, make loans from four Directors, and arrange extended payment terms with two suppliers of capital assets to carry it through this year, in spite of the slow sale of its second stock offering. Of the $80,000 authorized under this offering, only $31,000 has been sold. The Directors are continuing this offering in order to pay off the notes outstanding.*

In the offering circular, it was noted that a small number of individuals and firms were issued stock in compensation for services rendered and/or materials furnished. Sugarloaf was always more than a business enterprise—it was a community project.

One of the recipients was Jack Havey of Augusta, who had developed the earliest promotional materials,

**Left:** *Admiring an early trail map.* **Right:** *Ryan Fendler and Alice Baxter at the top of #3 T-Bar, 1957.*

including a brochure with the headline SUGARLOAF...IT'S THE GREATEST!! Several years later when it was my job to search for and hire an advertising agency to succeed AdVentures and to help put Sugarloaf on the map after the Gondola was installed, I turned to Jack and his imaginative crew to create our image and market the "Sugarloaf experience." He was finally able to actually make some money from the relationship as a paid professional. Parenthetically, Jack would help me promote Mount Snow and Saddleback as my career evolved. When I left the industry, I joined Jack as his partner in Ad-Media, and we were to spend more than ten fabulous years in the business together. Small world!

The Sugarloaf board of directors, orig-

inally nine visionaries, had evolved to include twenty-three members, including Amos Winter and the four original officers previously noted. They hailed from Maine and beyond, and represented a variety of backgrounds and interests:

Don Blanchard, Winthrop, Blanchard Associates

Fletcher Brown, Portland, Brown Motors, Inc.

Ben Butler, Farmington, Registrar of Stock, Lawyer, State Senator

George Cary, Bath, Bath Iron Works

Horace Chapman, Bangor, Manager, Bangor House

John Chapman, Portland, Principal, Waynflete School

H. King Cummings, Newport, Woolen Manufacturer

Ralph Goodwin, Auburn, Oculist

Bill Kierstead, Waterville, Dentist

George Mendall, Augusta, P.W. Brooks and Company

Herb Preston, Kingfield, Insurance

Allan Quimby, Bingham, Allan Quimby Veneer Company

Bob Scott, Orono, P.W. Brooks and Company

Scott Scully, Portland, Attorney for Maine Central Railroad

Rand Stowell, Dixfield,

Timberlands, Inc.
Art Sunderland, Lawrence,
Massachusetts, Bay State
Merchants National Bank
Bill Vaughan, Hallowell,
State Representative
Clarence Wyman, Kingfield,
Electrical Manufacturer

The summer of 1957 also marked the construction of a motel by Leo Tague, west of Route 27 in Carrabassett, marking the birth of the original Chateau des Tagues. Many a Sugarloafer in years to come would join the down-Maine revelry that abounded there, both in this location and at a later site across the road, after the original motel burned down in the summer of 1961. That same summer, Irv and Edna Judson, who operated the Unity House in Unity, broke ground for the Sugarloaf Motel. "Ma" Judson's home cooking would attract folks year-round, while Irv held forth in the basement bar.

The 1957–58 ski season began on December 14 and would continue uninterrupted until May 11 on near-record snow accumulations. In fact, at one point, the only way to get into the lift shack at the top of the #3 T-bar was to dig **down** to find the roof. Werner Rothbacher embarked on an ambitious Junior Program to develop young skiers, and several high-caliber races were conducted, culminating with the traditional Sugarloaf Schuss in April. That season, for the first time, the race was run as a downhill on the Tote Road, drawing the largest field in its history, including this author. I remember it well. Naysayers were grousing that a downhill couldn't be a real challenge on an intermediate trail. They were overlooking the fact that

two and a half miles is a long time in a tuck; that we were constantly accelerating on the steady pitch for the first mile; that Chicken Pitch and its god-awful transition were going to claim literally dozens of victims; and that the two rolls at the end of the trail after about three minutes were too much for the weary legs of

**Left:** *l-r: Stub and "Pooch" Taylor and Bert "Doc" Covert trudge up Winter's Way.*
**Right:** *The Werner Rothbacher Ski School.*

many of us who made it that far.

Intermediate trail? Just ask the then-young Icky Webber of Farmington, who won the event **averaging** better than sixty miles an hour!

It was becoming clear that the 800 and 400 passengers per hour (respectively) of the two lifts was insufficient to meet the demands of an increasing number of skiers, and the now-legendary waiting lines were stretching across the trails at the base of each lift. (Mazes, believe it or not, had not yet been invented.) During the summer of 1958, work was undertaken immediately after the area closed on May 11 to increase the capacity of the lower lift to alleviate congestion, and a small, barn-like structure was built at the top of the upper T-bar as protection against lift-stopping winds.

Another $10,000 was spent straightening, surfacing, and generally improving the access road, an additional parking lot was graveled, and the existing lots were improved.

The 1958–59 season began with Rothbacher and his staff of Austrian experts returning, as well as the hiring of someone to head up the Junior Program: Roger Page from Stowe, Vermont. Roger, who would later lead the effort to develop Saddleback in Rangeley, and become a ski school director / retailer extraordinaire there, had visited Sugarloaf on a couple of occasions: coaching the Junior Girls Team from Stowe at a race the previous winter, chaperoned by his wife, Patsy; and again during the summer to see about moving to the area, because he was overwhelmed by the potential he saw in the region. A chance meeting with Harvey Boynton resulted in his buying a house on Freeman Ridge in Kingfield.

An expanded novice slope that had been cut and groomed during the summer proved to be extremely popular among beginners who wanted to avoid the heavily traveled trails. The Mountain was once again blessed with the kind of snowfall that people were coming to expect of Sugarloaf, with opening day on December 6 and uninterrupted operation through April 23.

### THE BASE AREA RELOCATED

During the summer of 1959, the entire base area was relocated about 250 vertical feet down the mountain; a new two-story Lodge was constructed; and a 1,674-foot, 625-passengers-per-hour T-bar was installed to service the 15-acre beginners' area in front of the new Lodge, on terrain occupied by the original parking lots. New parking lots capable of accommodating nearly 1,000 vehicles were bulldozed and graveled west of the new Lodge,

and—of course—the access road was improved. (This is not a recording!)

Harvey Boynton moved his shop into a separate building with a large, south-facing roof that came to be called "Boynton's Beach," where spring skiers could bask in the afternoon sun and enjoy the company of old and newfound friends.

*Upper left:* Jack Havey's artwork promoting the mountain. **Lower left:** The original board of directors; l–r: George Mendall, Amos, Bill Vaughn, Rand Stowell, Bob Scott, Arthur Sunderland, King Cummings, "Bunny" Bass, George Cary, Fletcher Brown, Bill Kierstead, Horace Chapman, Dick Bell, Don Blanchard. **Right:** Ed Muskie gets a lesson from Werner Rothbacher.

During the 1959–60 season, 185 inches of snow fell, and more and more skiers discovered this mighty mountain, leading up to another very busy summer of improvements. A new wing, larger than the original section, was added to the east end of the Base Lodge. And several hundred feet farther to the east, a new 4,600-foot lift line was surveyed, cut, and bulldozed, in preparation for the installation of a fourth T-bar to be installed the following summer.

The grooming fleet grew to two, as another Tucker Sno-Cat was added. The upper trails were further groomed, and the Double Bitter was cut, paralleling the Tote Road from top to bottom, with a series of rolls, turns, and pitches that have made this 25-foot-wide trail a favorite among many Sugarloafers to this day.

On July 18, the newly formed Bigelow Corporation—whose principals included Harvey Boynton, Alden MacDonald, Wadsworth Hinds, and George "Tim" Terry—purchased the remaining lands of the 2,000-acre Merrow lot south of Route 27 and east of the access road, for a second home development to be called Sugarloaf Village.

Once again, the Mountain was blessed with plentiful snow during the 1960–'61 season. The Junior National Championships were moved to Sugarloaf from Stowe due to icy conditions there, and the Ski Club distinguished itself in the conduct of this important race—and on very short notice. It would not be the last important race that would be moved from another location because of Sugarloaf's combination of reliable snow and a group of experienced and dedicated race

officials, always ready to pitch in.

Thus ended the last ski season of the decade, and the realization of a dream—a foundation had been created for a world-class ski resort in Maine.

**Upper left and above:** *"Let it snow!"* **Lower left:** *Judson's opens for business.*

**Above:** *King Cummings (left) and Bob Scott.*
**Right:** *Amos and Alice Winter at the ticket window.* **Right:** *The new base lodge, located farther down the mountain.*

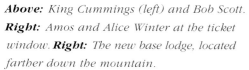

# Becoming Sugarloaf/USA:
## *1961–1971*

In April 1961, after returning to the United States from a postgraduate stint studying literature at the University of Stockholm, in Sweden, I went to Sugarloaf to race in the Schuss and to get in some spring skiing. It was apparent there was going to be plenty of it, as more than 200 inches of snow would fall on the Mountain that season. All the trails were open and well covered, and there was every indication that the area would likely stay open well into May.

My old Bowdoin buddy, Bruce Chalmers, and several other friends and I were staying as Dick Bell's guests in his old Bigelow Station at the end of the access road on the weekend of the Schuss. Come Sunday afternoon, my friends were getting ready to leave, and we had to move out of the Station. I didn't want to leave, but I had a problem: I had no place to stay, and all the money I had in the world was the five dollars that Bruce had generously given to me. Fate intervened in the person of Wayne Wibby from Bangor, now a successfully retired oral surgeon.

Wayne was on the Ski Patrol and had the misfortune of breaking an ankle on that very Sunday. As I was chatting with Amos in the Base Lodge at the end of the day, he asked me what I was doing for the rest of the season, and if I'd be interested in taking Wayne's patrolman job. I replied, "Sure, but I don't have any place to stay." Amos smiled and told me to go down and see Irv Judson at the Sugarloaf Motel. Wayne had been tending bar for Irv, which qualified him for a bunk in the bunkroom. I did, and the rest, as they say, is history.

## TWO MORE LIFTS INSTALLED

The timing of my arrival couldn't have been more propitious, as the summer of 1961 was going to be a busy one on the Mountain, with the planned installation of T-bars #4 and #5, and a rebuild of #3. When the ski season drew to a close in early May, Amos was assembling a crew for the

***Above:*** *The author (left) and Karl Krieger at the top of Sluice.* ***Below:*** *Sugarloaf.*

summer, and he asked if I'd be interested in staying on. I eagerly agreed. Although I had never seriously considered skiing as a career, my graduate work in literature suggested to me that I probably wasn't cut out for the cloistered life of a teacher. I really needed to be around some action. I was enthralled with Sugarloaf and everything that was happening there, and sensed I could be in on the early stages of something very special. It had been seven years since my first visit, and the progress made in those intervening years indicated that a great ski area was in the process of being built. Here was a chance to be a part of it. I took the job, and convinced Irv and Edna to let me stay on and tend bar in return for room and board.

The 1960–61 ski season had been such a successful one in terms of both snowfall and business that early in the first week of May, when the directors were meeting in Augusta, they decided to offer free skiing on May 6 and 7, the final weekend. Hundreds showed up to enjoy ideal summit-to-base conditions.

The summer of 1961 was hot and dry, perfect for digging lift-tower foundation holes, pouring concrete, and erecting steel for the two Constam T-bar lifts. In addition to installing the lifts, we cut Upper and Lower Ramdown, Widowmaker, Buckboard, and the Pole Line (actually the power line to the lower terminal of #5 T-bar), adding nearly five miles of new trails. The lower lift, #4, would be the longest lift on the mountain to date. Its lower terminal was located a few hundred feet to the east of the Base Lodge, and the upper terminal was placed nearly 4,600 feet up the mountain, with a vertical rise of 935 feet. It would be capable of loading 774 passengers per hour.

T-bar #5, in tandem with #4, and with a loading area slightly downhill and to the east of the unloading area of the lower lift, would be 3,160 feet long, rising 935 feet, and would load 630 skiers per hour.

My first lessons in trail layout, taught by Professor Winter, were an experience that has stayed with

me to this day. Amos would start down the fall line through the woods from the beginning of a planned trail, and Stub Taylor and I would position ourselves about 20 feet on either side of him, equipped with large balls of twine. Amos would work his way down the mountain, with Stub and I maintaining our 20-foot separation from him, marking our descent with twine stretched from tree to tree behind us. These lines of twine were the outside edges of the trail we would later cut by hand.

Amos had learned something about trail design by working with Sel Hannah earlier on the Mountain, but, more importantly, he was guided by his own experience and his instincts as a skier. He had realized the original Winter's Way was flawed because much of it was angling across the fall line, making it difficult to ski. This design also allowed skiers to force snow to the downhill side of the trail—something Amos called "slabbing," which he assiduously avoided in every trail he helped lay out after the original one.

Amos placed turns, whenever possible, in the natural flat areas in the terrain before turning again to rejoin the fall line. Many a time, after bushwhacking down the mountain for a few hundred feet, Stub and I would have to head back up the hill, re-balling our twine, because Amos had decided he didn't care for the section we had just completed, and had decided to try a different route.

To this day, Widowmaker and Ramdown—as well as Boom Auger, Bubble Cuffer, and Wedge, which we laid out in a subsequent summer—remain among my favorite trails anywhere. Not just because they bring back such fond memories, but because, for the most part, they don't "slab"!

## NAMING THE TRAILS

It's appropriate here to talk about the derivation of all the trail names at Sugarloaf. When the trails that would be named Narrow Gauge and Sluice were laid out and cut, Amos spearheaded the decision to make logging lingo the

*The author (right) welcomes Governor John Reed.*

theme. Not only were there plenty of terms aptly suited to ski trails, but naming the trails for logging terms emphasized the history and tradition of Maine's Tall Timber region. Once the thematic decision was made, one might suspect that a glossary of terms would have been sought out to provide a list of potential names. (Years later, a Google search would have provided such a resource.) Such was not the case. A few minutes with Amos, Stub, Leonard Cyr, and a few other locals produced more than enough potential trail names, given the rich vernacular of the logging and timber industry.

We started a file of such names, and definitions, to wit:

▲ Binder—a springy wooden pole holding a log raft together
▲ Birch Hook—similar to a pulp hook, but with a sharper point for use with hardwood
▲ Boardwalk—plank walkways on log booms
▲ Boom Auger—a hand-operated drill used to make holes in boom logs through which the boom chains would be run
▲ Bubble Cuffer—a logger who walked on logs in the water
▲ Buckboard—both a four-wheeled open carriage and a bulletin board for keeping track of work accomplished
▲ Bucksaw—a saw with an H-shaped frame, tightened with a turnbuckle
▲ Bull—the boss in a logging operation
▲ Candy Side—the crew with the best equipment
▲ Chaser—the man who hooks and unhooks logs from a choker
▲ Choker—wire cable used for yarding logs
▲ Cribworks—both a platform for loading logs onto a train and, when filled with rocks in a river, used to tether and separate logs in a drive (you can still see several of them in the Kennebec, just above Madison)
▲ Cruiser—a timber-volume estimator
▲ Double Bitter—a double-edged ax

▲ Double Runner—a sled with two sets of tracks

▲ Flume—a water trough for sliding logs down steep pitches

▲ Glancer—a log used to keep logs on a skidding trail (also called a Fender Skid, Breastwork Log, or Sheer Skid)

▲ Haulback—a cable returning chokers back to the wood source

▲ Hayburner—a horse

▲ Haywire—originally the wire binding a bale of hay, but more commonly a term referring to anything that isn't just right

▲ High Rigger—the daring logger who tops trees and connects the high lead wire

▲ Jagger—a sharp sliver of wire rope

▲ Jill Poke—a log in a stream at an odd angle, apt to cause a jam; also an awkward person

▲ Landing—the place where logs are gathered to roll them into the river

▲ Narrow Gauge—a 2-foot-wide train track

▲ Peavey—a steel-pointed wooden pole with a lever, used for turning logs

▲ Pick Pole—a 10- to 16-foot pole used for maneuvering logs in the water

▲ Ramdown—a steep hole, where horses were apt to be rammed from behind by their sleds

▲ Ripsaw—a saw for cutting logs lengthwise

▲ Scoot—a set of double-ended runners used for hauling logs

▲ Skidder—a yarding and loading engine

▲ Slasher—a large gas saw

▲ Sluice—a chute to move logs down steep grades, with the help of water

▲ Snubber—a braking device on sleighs

▲ Spillway—an opening to let logs through a dam

▲ Springboard—a small platform on which loggers stand while cutting a tree

▲ Spurline—a side railroad line

▲ Tohaul—a log jam

▲ Tote Road—a road going into the woods from a logging camp

▲ Wedge—a triangular-shaped piece of steel used in a saw cut in a tree to help direct the fall

▲ Whiffletree—a bar of wood used to hitch horses to a buckboard or to logs

▲ Widowmaker—a tree or branch blown down by the wind

▲ Windrow—a row of brush on the side of a logging road

Not only were we able to get T-bars #4 and #5 installed and operating for the 1961–62 ski season, but we also rebuilt the #3 T-bar to increase its capacity from 400 to 650 skiers per hour.

The summer of 1961 is especially memorable to me for two other very important reasons. It seems I was being eyed as a possible assistant, and perhaps even successor, to Amos. As the summer wound down, the board asked me if I'd consider staying on as assistant manager. Did they really need to ask? Of course I would. And I did.

The second reason the summer meant so much to me was because that was the year I really got to know, and love, Amos and Alice and their daughter, Christine. It seems Amos liked my energy and work ethic and my eagerness to learn everything he had to teach me. He also liked the company of someone who'd join him virtually every day after working ten hours on the mountain in a set or two of tennis on his wonderfully manicured clay court, next to his camp on Tufts Pond. Since it had to be rolled by hand, he appreciated a young volunteer who was willing to drag the heavy roller around every day after we scuffed up the surface.

**Upper left:** *The expanded base lodge.* **Lower left:** *Werner's ski school grows.* **Right:** *Sugarloaf, 1963.*

The reward for all of this was getting to know this remarkable couple as not only friends, but as almost surrogate parents. Having grown up without a father, I found in Amos a role model that had always been missing from my life. I enjoyed sharpening my relatively dull tennis skills under the watchful eye of a very accomplished mentor, and then concluding every match with a swim in the pond, followed by a family-style dinner exquisitely prepared by their sister-in-law, Hilda Winter, at Deer Farm Camps a few hundred yards away. We'd cap our evenings with a drive to Madison, the closest place for soft-serve ice cream and Amos's particular culinary fetish: a very thick coffee frappe. He got the

same frappe, served by the same girl, at the same dairy bar on the corner every night, yet he would, without fail, always offer the following admonishment: "Now don't beat the s— out of it!" I loved that man.

As busy as we were on the Mountain that summer, nearly doubling its size and uphill capacity, and continuing to improve the access road by removing

the large bend in the road near the swamp and adding much-needed additional gravel to a major portion of the road, exciting things were happening down in the Valley as well.

## POWER TO THE VALLEY

Leo Tague's motel, on the west side of Route 27, burned down early in the summer and was rebuilt across the road by Emery Hall from New Portland. Tague, one of the original paid members of the Ski Patrol and a sometime ski instructor, was spearheading an effort to get electricity to the valley. At that time Rangeley Power Company's lines extended only as far south as the access road. He and the Judsons were generating their own power for their commercial operations. About fifty additional people had homes or camps between Sugarloaf and Ken Packard's house below Spring Farm. In a letter dated August 21, 1961, Leo polled the property owners regarding their interest in the following way:

*TO PROSPECTIVE CUSTOMERS ON THE CARRABASSETT EXTENSION:*

*The Rangeley Power Company has assured us that if enough prospective customers evidence an interest, they will construct an extension of their electric power line from its present terminus near the Somerset Telephone Company building below the Sugarloaf Mountain access road to the Kenneth Packard property, which is below my motel a mile or so. If we obtain an adequate and prompt response to this letter, we have been assured that work will be started right away and completed in time for this winter's use.*

*In view of the rather large investment required to construct this line, the power company is asking that each residential customer agree to purchase a minimum of five dollars' worth of*

***Above:*** *Maine skiing icon Dana Wallace ready to compete in the Up the Mountain Road Race.*
***Below:*** *Ready. Set. Go!*

*electricity per month for a period of sixty months, after which time the monthly minimum would be at the regular rate, currently $1.50 per month. All future customers coming on the new line within this sixty-month period would pay the minimum five-dollar charge for the balance left of the sixty months.*

*Will you please complete the form enclosed evidencing your interest, or lack of interest, in this proposed service and return it to me as soon as possible?*

Included in that appeal were some names that would be closely linked to Sugarloaf's growth in years to come, including Robert Bass, Dr. Harry Brinkman, George Cary, "Chendy" Chenard, Dr. Arthur Corriveau, Towers Daggett, Brent Darlington, Dr. Dana Dingley, Ralph Gould, Herb Hoefler, Dave Horn, Dr. Maynard Irish, Dr. Bill Kierstead, Lew Krieger, George Mendall, Steve Monaghan, "Bud" Ragon, "Skip" Skaling, Arthur Sunderland, and John White.

The response was affirmative, and the line was extended. The timing couldn't have been better. The boom in camp building was really beginning to accelerate on lots leased from the State and from Dead River Company in Spring Farm, Poplar Stream, and the Valley Crossing area, and along Route 27 between Carrabassett and Stratton.

At the same time Dick Berry and his Rangeley Power Company were electrifying the valley, Kenton Quint of the Somerset Telephone Company in North Anson, the local phone service provider, authorized the creation of the Bigelow exchange (237), with eight subscribers.

Up on the Mountain, trails were further groomed, which was prescient, since snow conditions during the 1961–62 season were less than ideal. Frozen granular was the prevailing surface through the entire month of January. While some might think the term "frozen granular" is a euphemism for "ice," I would remind them of a wonderful comment Roger Page once made to me when we were together at Saddleback.

We were looking out at a particularly shiny surface in front of the base lodge there one day, and he asked me if I'd like to take a run. I said, "Sure, but it's all ice." To which he replied, "John, if there ain't fish under it, it ain't ice!" Clear confirmation that for those of us who dared to get into the ski business, the glass was always half full.

And in that vein, our old friend and Sugarloaf institution, Brud Folger, tells a story about seeing Amos in the Base Lodge on a day when the sun was reflecting off the hard surface of the Bunny Slope. Brud asked him, "How's your new man Christie working out?" (It's important to note that I was living in a closet-size room in the basement of the Base Lodge that winter. In addition to cleaning the bathrooms, I was responsible for calling the radio stations each morning, starting at about 4:30 A.M., to report the snow conditions for the day.) Amos responded to Brud: "Oh, I don't know. The damn fool's calling it packed powder, and just look at it *glisten!*"

During the summer of 1962, Charlie and Elinor Clark, assuring Emery Hall another busy year in construction, built the beautiful Capricorn Lodge (now the home of Carrabassett Valley Academy); the aforementioned Brud Folger and Billy Jones (Stratton native and son of the proprietor of Jones General Store) built the Sugarloaf Sauna (now Hug's Restaurant); and housing growth in the valley continued apace. I joined that trend by leasing a piece of land (for $50 a year) on a bend in the river by the upper entrance to Spring Farm, in order to build a small chalet during the following summer with the help of Dave Rollins and Wes Sanborn. They were refurbishing an old barn that was to become the Red Stallion Inn, and developing a virtual village of A-frames on the north side of the Carrabassett, later called Carrabassett Village.

*Amos and Alice Winter, a true reflection of Sugarloaf.*

During that same summer, George Cary was elected president of the Sugarloaf Mountain Corporation, an entity that by now had five T-bars, two base lodges, an Austrian ski school, a ten-person ski patrol, and extensive first-aid equipment. Additionally, the fleet of rolling stock now included a bulldozer, mowing tractor, and two Tucker Sno-Cats. All of the lifts were equipped with automatic safety devices and were powered by electric motors (although the two original lifts retained their gas engines for auxiliary use, if necessary).

I remember 1962 for another reason: It was the year that banjo player Jud Strunk, from Buffalo, New York, arrived. He and a piano player named Gil Krause were entertaining that spring at the Red Stallion. Jud fell in love with the area, and almost before he (or any of the rest of us, for that matter) knew it, he had become the first director of the newly formed Sugarloaf Area Association. This was a collective of commercial interests, the Mountain, and other interested parties who banded together to promote the area, year-round.

The 1962–63 ski season, which ended on April 21, saw a continuation of the growth in skier visits, and more and more individuals and families were becoming true Sugarloafers by buying season passes and investing in area property.

And speaking of season passes, it wasn't until the following season that photo passes were available. Up until then, every season pass holder was issued a day pass. The inconvenience was minimal, since Amos and Alice, and their number-one helper in the ticket booth, Tom Pease, knew every single pass holder by name. Identification was never an issue.

During the summer of 1963, a third section was added to the east end of the Base Lodge, which architecturally balanced the original west section. This addition provided more space for visitors on the second floor, while the basement accommodated a nursery, to be ably run by Joyce Pease, Tom's wife, and an expanded first-aid and ski-patrol room. In addition, Sugarloaf's first news bureau was established—actually, just a mimeograph machine on a folding table. I constantly ran off press releases to keep the media aware of important (and even unimportant) things that we were up to on the Mountain and in the surrounding area. Between Jud Strunk and me, hardly a day went by that some news didn't emanate from our separate mimeograph machines at the mountain and the Area Association office down in the valley.

Jud, Billy Jones, and I were living in a rented chalet next to the Sugarloaf Inn for the summer, and the three of us, along with our guitar-playing best friend, Bill Blake, formed a singing group (really, Jud and three amateur supporters) aptly named (we thought) "The Sugarloafers." We went on to entertain throughout that summer at

*Left:* Putting in the gondola towers. **Right:** *Keystone's S-58 Sikorsky flies a gondola tower to its foundation.*

venues like Louie's Steak House in East Winthrop and the Saddleback Motor Inn, as well as at various consumer ski shows in the fall.

This fall marked another of life's memorable moments . . . unpleasant as it was. It is said that everyone in my generation can remember where they were when they heard that President John F. Kennedy had been shot. Well, I was in the ladies' room in the Sugarloaf Base Lodge. I had been working all day up on the trails, and when I came down to the lodge, I noticed the ladies' room door was being held open by a can of paint. Amos was inside, painting the floor. I stuck my head in to say hi to him, and I'll never forget his words: "Hey, John, hope you weren't planning to vote for Kennedy . . . they just shot him."

And, by a serendipitous coincidence, not only did President Kennedy die

in November of 1963, but so did the career of one Vaughn Meader, a Maine boy who had gained fame and fortune with his recording, "The First Family," in which he imitated to perfection JFK's voice, accent, and inflection. The Sugarloafers were his opening act when he had performed at Lakewood earlier in the summer. Although he continued to entertain for the rest of his life, including a season at Sugarloaf in the early 1970s, he never again attained national recognition.

Also that summer, the Somerset Telephone Company had leased a small tract of land on the summit to construct a microwave relay station and, more importantly from the ski area's standpoint, an access road on a strip of land that ran parallel to the Tote Road from the base area to the summit. This road would prove invaluable in subsequent years, as it would be used to transport construction material for future lifts and the massive upper terminal for the Gondola. The road even became the venue for a series of foot races in future summers, called the "Sugarloaf Up-the-Mountain Road Race," a Strunk/Christie production. The road did double duty as a ski trail. It was first named Quint's Road after Kenton Quint, the owner of Somerset Telephone Company, and was later renamed Binder to join the logging lexicon.

The lower terminal of the original T-bar was moved downhill from its location just above the original Base Lodge, which was demolished that summer, to a spot slightly below what is now the lower terminal of the Double Runner Chair. The additional 1,200 feet of length necessitated a larger cable; hence, a wider-diameter, 8-foot bull wheel replaced the original 6-footer, and all of the towers were widened. No small job, but well worth the effort, as skiers could now ride from the base area to the snowfields on two lifts in tandem, as opposed to three.

The 1963–64 ski season began the day after Christmas and continued until April 13, on total snow accumulation of some 97 inches. Despite lower-than-average snowfall, Sugarloaf's grooming equipment was maintained by Don "Kid" Murray and his crew, and operated by Clayton Wilbur (whose wife, Hilma, assisted in the ticket office) and his grooming crew.

During the summer of 1964, the State would pave and modestly lengthen the Sugarloaf Regional Airport, which meant that pilots Joe Sewall, H. King Cummings, and others would not have to resort to taking off down Route 27 on spring afternoons. After a warm day of skiing, the slushy strip would be too soft for an airplane to taxi. This improvement marked the first real work done on the strip since the U.S. Army had built it in 1942 as an emergency landing field.

December of 1964 was unusually warm. I washed the free station wagon that Buick and Bud Nickerson from Farmington had given to us for promotional purposes outside the Base Lodge, in 60-degree weather on Christmas Day, with not a speck of snow on the ground. But by midnight it had started to snow, and we were able to open on the 29th, the latest date ever. And although only 77 inches of snow fell that winter, we operated until May 2, thanks to some traditional March and April storms.

## THE MIGHTY GONDOLA

The preceding two summers of only minimal construction on the Mountain allowed us to catch our breath from the frenetic and exhausting expansion pace of the previous few years and prepare ourselves—physically, emotionally, and

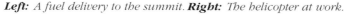
*Left:* A fuel delivery to the summit. **Right:** The helicopter at work.

financially—for what was to become the defining event in Sugarloaf's transformation from Sugarloaf Mountain to SUGARLOAF/USA.

That event—the installation of what was to be referred to as "The Mighty Gondola"—was preceded by several years of planning under the guiding hand of George Cary, an engineer by training and profession.

We had surveyed and cut a lift line during the summer of 1964, even before a decision had been made as to exactly what type of lift or manufacturer would be selected. When I say we surveyed the lift line, I should say, more accurately, that I surveyed it. I've since been recognized as the fool who located the lower terminal in the middle of a brook. Here's what happened: Since my first summer at Sugarloaf, I had been the designated transit operator, lining up the T-bar towers every fall as they got moved around each year by the frost. It was important that they be aligned so that the cable would stay on the wheels as much as possible. Amos had bestowed this distinction upon me. He must have assumed that because I was the one guy on the summer crew who had gone to college, I must know something—overlooking the fact that I had majored in English and didn't even know which end of a transit I was supposed to look into!

Despite that paucity of competence, Amos gave me the job of laying out the new lift line. We determined the location for an upper terminal, and I sighted down to a spot in the vicinity of the Base Lodge. Swinging the transit up, I was looking directly at the remains of the fire tower on Avery Peak on Bigelow. What a fortuitous coincidence, I thought, since as I worked my way down the mountain, laying out the centerline, I could use the tower for alignment. I was so excited about this development that it never occurred to me to check to see exactly where that would place the lower terminal. Oh, well....It all worked out—except we had to move the brook (by bulldozing a new channel)!

A quick story about the cutting of the Gondola line: Among the crew we assembled was an experienced woodsman from Kingfield, one Leonard Cyr, who had been working all his life in the woods and had, in fact, been part of the crew that cut the Flagstaff Lake flowage. He arrived the first day on the job with his own ax, and I told him he didn't have to use it since we had plenty of them. His reply has stayed with me: "Thanks, but this is my favorite. I've had it about twenty-five years. Of course I've had a bunch of different handles, and I've replaced the head three or four times." Leonard stayed after that summer and became not only a valued member of our year-round staff, but also a special

favorite of mine for his willingness to take on any job, at any time, in any weather.

George Cary and the directors

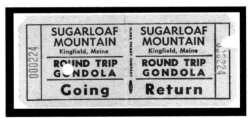

*Left: The "Mighty Gondola" is born.* **Upper right:** *Amos and the author waiting for the helicopter to snatch up another tower.* **Lower right:** *A ticket for one ride on the gondola— summer or winter.*

had agreed on a couple of things about a prospective lift: It should be an aerial lift, and, as such, it should probably be enclosed. Riders would need protection from the elements, especially for that portion above the timberline. So a gondola-type lift made the most sense, and one with four-passenger cabins seemed like the best choice, as opposed to the two-passenger version in operation at Wildcat

Mountain. This configuration would be more apt to attract summer traffic, they reasoned. Another argument in favor of the four-passenger version was the slightly higher number of passengers that could be loaded per hour and, even more important, the weight of the larger cabin would render it somewhat more impervious to swaying in the predictable northwest winds, especially above the timberline.

The final decision to commit to the purchase of a German Polig-Heckel-Bleichert (PHB) lift was solidified by a visit from King Cummings, George Cary, and me to a similar lift that had recently been installed at Park City, Utah. One of the convincing factors was that the Park City lift was in two sections. It had a mid-station through which cars could pass when the lift was operating to the summit, but which could also be used as the upper terminal when weather or skiing conditions mitigated against operating all the way to the top. Conversely, one could operate only the upper section, which would prove to be the case on Sugarloaf years later, during the lift's final seasons. George Cary knew that there'd be

**Left:** *George Mendall in the snowfields.*
**Right:** *Harry and Martha Baxter in front of the sign that Harry built.*

days, perhaps many of them, when we wouldn't be able (or even want) to put skiers on the summit, so this option sealed the deal.

The summer of 1965 may well go down in history as the most important since the summer of 1950, when the original trail was cut. A few guys from Maine would erect an 8,430-foot aerial lift, rising 2,350 feet up the steep north face of the state's second-highest mountain—a truly Herculean task.

Every tower was preassembled in the parking lot and flown onto its pre-poured foundation by a Sikorsky S-58 helicopter, operated by Keystone Helicopters from Pennsylvania. That particular aircraft was rated to lift 4,000

pounds to 4,000 feet—a task it was called upon to do often that summer.

Assembling and erecting the complex structure proved to be especially daunting for our English- and French-speaking crew, since the blueprints and manuals were all in German. We thought our translation problems would be solved upon the midsummer arrival of Wilfred Eschenauer, an engineer supplied by the factory. His command of German, it goes without saying, was perfect, but he neither understood nor spoke a single word of English (although a summer with us did teach him a unique version of that language).

So we were back at square one, until our salvation arrived. George Cary, who spent Monday through Friday at his real job as an engineer at Bath Iron Works, had an associate there who was fluent in both English and German. On Sunday nights George would deliver to him the working documents we'd be using two weeks hence, and when he returned to Sugarloaf on Friday night,

with him were our marching orders for the next week, spelled out in perfect English.

It's difficult to capture, and to even remember clearly, the magnitude of that summer's project. The concrete for the upper terminal, and all of the lift towers above the mid-station, was mixed in a makeshift batching plant comprised of an old transit-mix truck that was dragged to the summit by Tiger White from Carthage and his D-8 Caterpillar.

And that's not all that was transported to the 4,190-foot elevation on the Mountain. Consider this: Up that rudimentary access road was hauled some 400 tons of pre-stressed concrete slabs for the terminal building's walls and floors; 7 tons of tinted, double-paned plate-glass windows; 23 tons of 3-inch-thick western cedar for the roof; and 60 tons of structural steel. All of this for the construction of a building to house not only the lift mechanisms, but also first-aid and restaurant facilities as well.

When operations began for the 1965–66 ski season on the weekend before Christmas, we were still pouring the concrete foundation for the upper terminal. Don Fowler, Sugarloaf regular, and a Bowdoin classmate of George Cary's son, George, remembers "volunteering" to man the kerosene-fired Salamander heaters on frigid December nights on the summit as we worked to prevent the concrete from freezing as it cured.

Late in January, fifty brightly painted four-passenger gondolas, each emblazoned with the ubiquitous triangular Sugarloaf logo, began rotating on the nearly 8,500-foot aerial lift. Although it was a couple of months late, to those of us who were involved in its construction, it was tear-jerkingly miraculous to see it operating at all. "The Year of the Mighty Gondola" had arrived. I'll remember forever the efforts of Stub, Leonard, and Joe West and our stalwart crew. But most of all, I'll always be grateful that we had Hazen McMullen to guide and inspire us with his native intelligence, skill, experience, good humor, and, most of all, his seemingly superhuman strength.

That phrase—THE YEAR OF THE MIGHTY GONDOLA—was the headline

*Upper left: l–r: The author and Jill Christie, and Martha and Harry Baxter. **Lower left:** Sugarloaf's beautiful people: l–r: "Buffy" Bell, Anne Bell, Jill Christie, Harvey Packard, and Jamie Corriveau. **Right:** Services at the Richard Bell Chapel.*

in our promotional materials that year, and the creation of Jack Havey and his imaginative group of advertising copywriters and designers at Ad-Media on State Street in Augusta. His assignment was to tell the world that Sugarloaf had arrived as a major destination. As we strategized with Jack about how we'd do this, he asked

Walt Ernst, a gifted copywriter on his staff, to help us.

Walt can be credited with conceiving the identity of SUGARLOAF/USA —in retrospect, a stroke of genius. It immediately implied size, scale, and international stature. With the help of some considerable media dollars, people from all over were beginning to hear about, and consider visiting, Sugarloaf.

Years later, I had the good fortune to introduce Bunny Bass at the banquet celebrating his induction into the Maine Ski Hall of Fame, in its inaugural class of 2003. I reminded the audience that Bunny had said, after the first year of the gondola's operation: "That lift may not have gotten a lot of people to the summit, but it sure got a lot of people from Boston to Sugarloaf."

I also have a strong suspicion that it was the notoriety of the gondola, and not my ability, which provoked my election in 1965 to the presidency of both the Sugarloaf Mountain Ski Club and the Maine Ski Council.

Down in the base area, people who had heretofore felt guilty about choosing skiing over church on Sunday morning began attending Sunday services at the Richard Bell Sugarloaf Interfaith Chapel, constructed during the summer of 1965 at the lower end of the parking lots, below the Base Lodge. The chapel rightly bore the name of the individual who not only single-handedly made it a reality, but who also tirelessly promoted Sugarloaf twenty-four hours a day. I'm proud that "Uncle Dick" became one of my closest friends and most ardent supporters throughout my entire skiing career.

Once again, the Mountain operated into May, with 139 inches of recorded snowfall, allowing more than three months of gondola operation despite the late start during that initial season. Word

**Left:** *Springtime on Harvey Boynton's "Beach."* **Right:** *Harvey Boynton*

began to spread.

There was only one unfortunate mishap on the Gondola during its initial season of operation, and that was the disengagement of one of the cabins just as it departed the mid-station, headed toward the summit. The splice in the upper section's cable was passing through the mid-station just as the car was launched manually. The increased diameter of the splice prevented complete engagement, so as it headed uphill, it began to slide back before falling completely off the cable, tumbling a short distance in a trough of snow back to the mid-station.

In the cabin were regulars Herb Hoefler and Nel Plattner, both scraped up a little, but otherwise none the worse for wear. With them was Bob Kelleter from the *Bangor Daily News,* who was also unscathed, except for the fact that his new Bogner stretch pants were badly ripped. Bob encountered Amos in the Base Lodge and demanded restitution. Amos pointed at the large toilet-tissue box located at the end of the Ski School counter, which comprised our Lost and Found Department, and said, "Why don't you look in there and see what you can find." Nowadays, he'd be offered a complete new outfit, a lifetime season pass, and college tuition for all of his children, just to avoid a lawsuit— though Bob Kelleter, in fact, did not sue.

During the summer of 1966, Dick and Mary Fountain arrived in the area and built the Lumberjack Lodge, today a dormitory for Carrabassett Valley Academy (CVA) students. On the Mountain, while we caught our collective breaths after the frenetic pace of the past twelve months, we did move ahead on one very important front. Since the board had named me general manager, to succeed Amos, I had the opportunity to consider applicants to run the Ski School, as Werner Rothbacher was moving on.

I drove down to Ossipee, New Hampshire, to interview Harry Baxter and to meet his wife, Martha, and their young children. Harry was a sort of one-man manager / ski school director / marketing department at Mount Whittier, and had evidenced an interest in coming to Sugarloaf. It only took a few minutes to convince me that Harry and Martha would be just the right fit for us. We offered him the Ski School position, and he accepted. They moved up during the summer, and Harry single-handedly built the large entrance sign with the suspended gondola, which stood for years at the end of the access road.

*Above:* The mountain's "youthful" management team; l–r: Hazen McMullen, Ted Jones, the author.
*Below:* Jean Hodgkins and Don Fowler climb up for some late-spring skiing.

Little did we know then that in a couple of years he'd be named general manager when I would leave Sugarloaf to go to Vermont. Years later he would move to Jackson Hole, Wyoming, where he concluded a distinguished career in the ski business. Well into his seventies now, he can still ski circles around most of us!

## THE NCAA CHAMPIONSHIPS

Also during that summer, countless hours were spent in preparation for the 1967 NCAA Intercollegiate Skiing Championships, for which Colby, Bates, Bowdoin, and the University of Maine were the collective successful bidders, with Sugarloaf to be the host site.

Point man, and our contact for the event, was John Winkin, then athletic director at Colby. We worked closely with his ski coach, Si Dunklee, in locating and developing the required Nordic facilities. Days on end were spent with the tireless coach, tromping through the woods north of the Carrabassett and along the old narrow gauge right-of-way of the abandoned Franklin and Megantic Railroad, which ceased operation in 1936. We also needed to find a site for (and construct) a 35-meter jump. The appropriate terrain was located up behind the Red Stallion, south of the Carriage Road between the Carrabassett and Dead rivers. It was very close, incidentally, to the dump for Jerusalem, the predecessor to the town of Carrabassett Valley. (The dump would gain its own notoriety in 1969 when *Playboy* magazine featured a two-page picture of the now-famous "Dump Party.")

This NCAA competition was the most significant one undertaken to date, and would be just the precursor to a long series of national and international competitions that continue to this day—and for which Sugarloaf has become a preeminent location of choice.

Although only 83 inches of snow fell during the

1966–67 ski season, the Mountain once again operated well into April, a testimony not only to the dependability of conditions, but also to the quality of the grooming.

There was plenty of snow to support the competitors in the inaugural World Heavyweight Ski Championships that year. How was such an event conceived, you may ask? I'll blame Bud Leavitt of WABI-TV and *Bangor Daily News* notoriety. We were in his Carrabassett Village A-frame, often the site of lively, spirits-induced conversation, when Bud suggested we ought to do something for his "overweight" peers. (Remember—this was in the era before politically correct speech.) We decided to create a race for people who were more than

**Above:** *Sugarloaf's fabled snow.* **Below:** *Sugarloaf makes it into Life magazine—in an ad for Moto-Ski.*

250 pounds, where participants would be given handicap points for every additional pound. The heavier they were, the better their odds of winning. But the quid pro quo was that the entry fee was also by the pound, so the heavier the racer, the higher the fee. We decided the fees would be donated to a charity, to be named by the winner.

Bud and I, incidentally, had become great friends as a result of my taking over, at his request, the *Outdoors with Bud Leavitt* show from 6:00 to 6:30 P.M. on Channel 5 in Bangor. I did this show each Saturday night in January for several years during the mid-sixties, providing live ski instruction (since videotape had not yet been invented) on a pile of snow in the studio parking lot. To this day, people talk to me about my attempts to ski on "Mount Hildreth."

Local heroes and favorites in the first World Heavyweight Ski Championship were University of Maine alumni, and professional football players, Roger Ellis and Thurlow Cooper—two large Sugarloaf regulars. In fact, my dear friend Rob Pfeiffer who worked on the Mountain with me the first summer I was there, has sworn to me that Amos would give him a free ticket to ski behind Roger and Thurlow to fill in their sitzmarks, so we wouldn't face the liability of losing another skier in one of them!

Up from Springfield, Massachusetts, came one John Truden, weighing in at 340 pounds. Truden vanquished the field in not only the first, but also every subsequent race, to become the undisputed World Heavyweight Ski Champion. (Years later, when I was running Mount Snow, John's home mountain, we put him on our payroll, in a uniform proclaiming his distinction for all to see. This because Walt Schoenknecht, the everyman owner of Mount Snow, wanted people to see that you didn't have to be shaped like our other paid ambassador, Suzy Chaffee, in order to enjoy skiing.)

The summer of 1967 was devoted to slope grooming and summertime maintenance projects. The ski season began auspiciously on December 9, the earliest opening in nine years; the early start was appreciated by skiers in general, and especially by the growing number of season pass holders. Harry Baxter was particularly adept at organizing and promoting the learn-to-ski experience, and increasingly large numbers of people were taking weeklong vacations at winter destinations. Who can blame them? Copy in our brochure that winter read, in part:

*And here's the best ski deal of all! Unlimited skiing, daily lesson, 10 meals and lodging Sunday night through Friday afternoon. Starts at $49.50!*

The 1967–68 ski season was a sparse year for snowfall, and the Mountain closed on Friday, April 5, the earliest closing date in its history. Despite the lack of snow, however, the Dead River Company moved forward aggressively during the summer of 1968, building roads and offering house lots for sale in Redington North, a spectacularly beautiful tract of land off Route 27 with glorious views of the entire ski area.

It was with obviously mixed feelings that in the fall of 1968, I answered the siren call of a larger ski area and the magnetism of its owner, and accepted the position of vice president and general manager of the Mount Snow Development Corporation in West Dover, Vermont. Walt Schoenknecht, its visionary founder, had built what he promoted as "The World's Largest Ski Area." This claim was based on the fact he was hosting 7,000 or more skiers on weekend days. In addition to the ski area, which Walt had started in 1954, his company owned three hotels and a golf course. Too much for a kid from Camden, Maine, to resist.

My departure proved fortuitous for Sugarloaf in two ways: First, it allowed Harry Baxter to assume management responsibilities under newly elected president H. King Cummings, for whom King's Landing would later be named; and, second, it apparently provoked the snow gods to look charitably upon the Mountain, dumping a record 347 inches of snow during a season that began for the first time ever in November, on the 10th, and lasted until the 11th of May—a full six months of skiing!

Crews had to dig out the T-bar terminals and the Gondola mid-station

*A practice run up the flag poles set up for the 1971 World Cup races; climbers l–r: "Barney" Thompson, Wesley McKague, Daniel Harkins.*

just to allow the lifts to operate, and the season goes down in memory as the most spectacular snow year in Sugarloaf's storied history. Sixty-seven inches of snow fell in one storm alone, and special equipment was brought in from Aroostook County by the State to render Route 27 passable.

### THE FIRST CHAIRLIFT INSTALLED

During the summer of 1969, the Mountain's first chairlift, Bucksaw, was erected on a shoulder to the west of Tote Road, opening up a whole new area of novice and intermediate terrain. Its upper terminal was placed at about the level of the top of Chicken Pitch, and the lower terminal was at roughly the elevation of the Base Lodge. More than a mile long and rising 1,200 vertical feet, the double chairlift would have a capacity of 945 passengers per hour, thus helping to alleviate congestion on the T-bars and the Gondola. Glancer, Scoot, and Horseshoe trails were cut and available for use during the upcoming season.

Also during that summer, the Dead River Company constructed a shopping complex called Valley Crossing at the intersection of Route 27 and the road across the river to Carrabassett Village and the Red Stallion.

The 1969–70 season opened on the weekend before Christmas, some 150 inches of snow fell during the season, and operations came to a close on April 26—another very successful year.

During the summer of 1970, the Sugarloaf Mountain Corporation pur-

*Lang Warren mastering the snowfields.*

chased the Sugarloaf Inn from the Pfeifles, and a 1,300-foot double chairlift, the Sawduster, was installed to transport guests of the Inn to the Base Lodge and to service the novice terrain between them. In addition, the first twenty condominiums were constructed and sold on the Mountain, and the owners, along with other Sugarloaf skiers, were rewarded with early snowfall, a December 5th opening, and more than 250 inches of snow before closing day on May 2.

### THE WORLD CUP

Ample snow was only one of the reasons the skiing-world's eyes were on Sugarloaf during the 1970–71 season. This was also the year the Mountain hosted, in the words of local writer Esther Perne a "Double-Barreled World Cup" race.

Esther captured the story in a recap she wrote for the 1999–2000 50th Anniversary Magazine of the Sugarloaf Mountain Ski Club, which read, in part:

*If anything can surpass hosting a World Cup, it's what Sugarloaf accomplished in 1971. With too much snow and too few beds, an eleventh-hour notice, and the fate of the entire season's award system hanging in the balance, this almost unknown "mom and pop" area not only held the prestigious World Cup and Tall Timber Classic, but it also unexpectedly ran the downhill events of the European Arlberg-Kandahar.*

*Two separate World Cup competitions and a total of six events was not what Sugarloaf anticipated for its debut in the arena of elite international competition. Nor was it seeking the instant fame, added publicity, and surge of spectators the additional events would involve.*

*But the mountain was potentially prepared. It had done its homework in World Cup readiness: two years of public relations, fund-raising, organization, and logistics. It had the snow so lacking in Europe, that for the first time in 43 years, the Arlberg-Kandahar couldn't be held. And, of the five final competition sites for the 1971 circuit, Sugarloaf, only, could offer downhill.*

This event contained enough drama for an entire book: international attention focused on Sugarloaf; copious snow and superb racing conditions; an unfortunate fire that destroyed the Swiss team's equipment; a once-in-a-lifetime chance for ski racing fans to see the world's elite competitors in action; and an opportunity to cheer on not only the American team, but also local members thereof as well.

**Left:** *The new sign built by Harry Baxter.*
**Right:** *The gondola in its heyday.*

The event saw the emergence of Italian slalom ace Gustavo Thoeni as the star to watch in international ski competition, as he widened his World Cup points lead following his stellar performance—including his first-ever top-ten finish in a downhill.

European competitors of whom Sugarloafers had previously only read about became familiar faces: Stefano Anzi, Eddie Bruggman, Henri Duvillard, Annie Famose, Isabel Mir, Annemarie Proell, Patrick Russel, Bernhard Russi, and Karl Schranz.

Cheers erupted and cowbells rang as down the courses sped American favorites: Bob Cochran and his sisters Marilyn and Barbara, Rick Chaffee, and Terry Palmer; and the loudest applause was saved for local favorites Gail Blackburn, Tim Skaling, and Steve Lathrop.

*Above: Paul Francon of St. Etiene, France, exchange student—Cony High School, Augusta, with Govenor Kenneth M. Curtis and Isabell Mir, of the French Team at World Cup, Sugarloaf, Feb. 70. **Right top:** Gustavo Thoeni. **Right bottom:** Stein Ericksen.*

As the *Waterville Morning Sentinel* noted in an editorial at the conclusion of the event:

*The World Cup races at Sugarloaf are now history—happy history—and Maine people can be proud of the way the Sugarloaf people, from top management to the students who helped pack the*

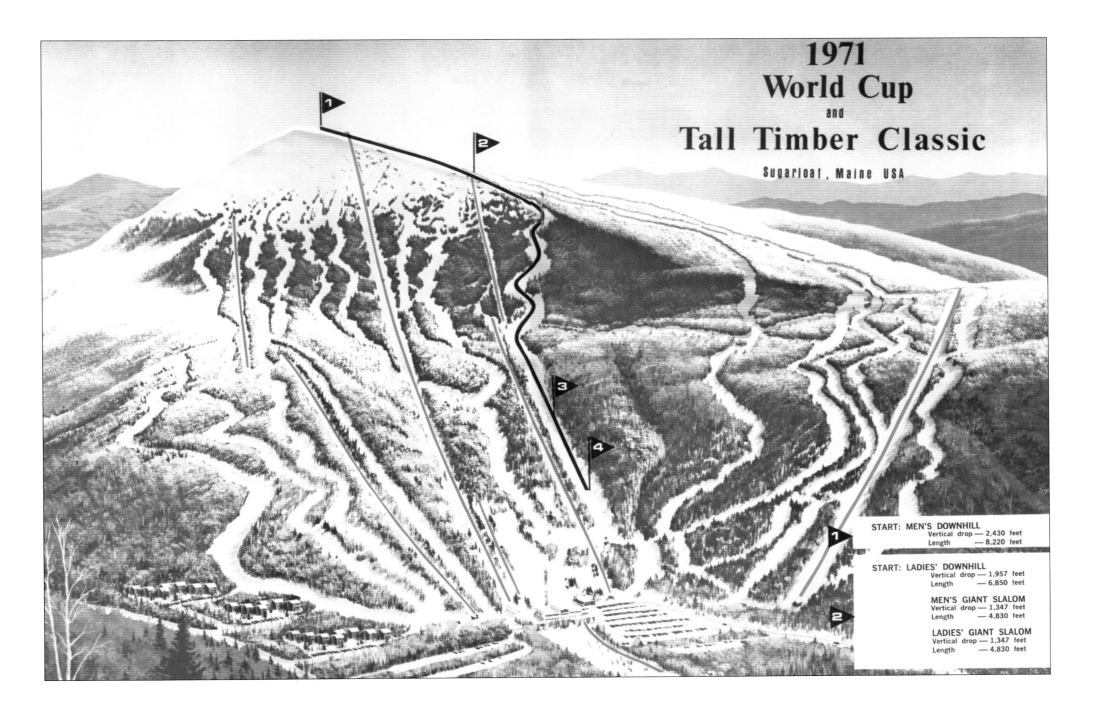

**1971**
**World Cup**
and
**Tall Timber Classic**

Sugarloaf, Maine USA

**START: MEN'S DOWNHILL**
Vertical drop — 2,430 feet
Length — 8,220 feet

**START: LADIES' DOWNHILL**
Vertical drop — 1,957 feet
Length — 6,850 feet

**MEN'S GIANT SLALOM**
Vertical drop — 1,347 feet
Length — 4,830 feet

**LADIES' GIANT SLALOM**
Vertical drop — 1,347 feet
Length — 4,830 feet

*Left:* Hazen McMullen—the man behind much of Sugarloaf's development. **Right:** Looking down the gondola line toward Bigelow.

*slopes, did their job. Maine's place in the skiing world has been firmly established.*

And so the 1970–71 ski season marked the arrival of Sugarloaf on the world stage, and the realization that it truly deserved the name: SUGARLOAF/USA.

# From Ski Area to Ski Resort:
## *1971–1980*

The decade of the 1970s was to mark the emergence of Sugarloaf as a true "destination" resort in the finest sense of the word. To be a destination where skiers go to stay for an extended period of time, the resort must have all of the necessary amenities (lodging, food, entertainment, and shopping), and it must allow visitors to leave their automobiles behind. They need to be able to walk or be bused to wherever they want to go during their stay. It also requires that there be a sense of place—in Gertrude Stein's words, "a there there"—populated by a community of people constituting a real town. The 1970s saw all of these needs met with an explosion of housing development on the Mountain and in the Valley, and the establishment of a real town with the incorporation of Carrabassett Valley in 1972.

The early years of the decade also served to remind everyone involved in the economics of the ski business, not only at Sugarloaf but elsewhere in the East, how fragile was the balance between success and failure, as both sparse snowfall and the first Arab oil embargo led to diminished traffic and a tenuous revenue stream.

The lack of natural snow in the early '70s actually had one positive outcome: It hastened the installation of a major snowmaking system in 1974, followed shortly thereafter with an investment in state-of-the-art grooming machinery.

Saddleback was, by odd coincidence, a beneficiary of the lack of snow at the beginning of the 1973 ski season.

In the fall of 1972, I left Mount Snow and reentered the ski business in Maine. I purchased Saddleback Mountain Ski Area in Rangeley with a company I'd formed, named (with a touch of hyperbole) the Big Rangeley Corporation. We ensured that the limited but functional snowmaking system installed on the beginners' area in front of the base lodge was brought up to snuff and made ready to start pumping snow as soon as the temperature allowed. This concept had proven itself at Mount Snow, where we were able to cover several hundred acres of skiable terrain with durable, man-made snow. We had seen firsthand the

*Don and Maryanne Pfeifles's Sugarloaf Inn.*

benefits derived from being able to guarantee skiing during the Christmas holidays, a hugely important kickoff for the season even if there was no natural snow.

As it turned out, December 1973 was a dry one—but cold. At Saddleback, we covered the small novice area serviced by a double chairlift with as much snow as we could in early December. When we opened in mid-December, we were ready for the Christmas rush. But we weren't quite ready for something else. You see, without any snowmaking capacity at that time, Sugarloaf lay brown and bare at Christmas. Gardner DeFoe and his Sugarloafer Ski Camp, filled up with eager young skiers, had to go somewhere, or else Gardner would have had to cancel his camp, lose the revenue, and chalk up the whole winter as a bust.

Gardner called, and we agreed to let them ski for what was practically nothing on some terrain that wasn't much more than that. But they were happy and the camp was salvaged; Saddleback was exposed to a lot of skiers who otherwise would never have visited; the bank that helped finance the area's purchase and development was delighted; and we sure sold a lot of hamburgers and hot chocolate!

But let's go back to the summer of 1971. The excitement of the World Cup was waning. Early in the spring, Chris Hutchins, son of the scion of the Dead River Company and point man on its considerable activities in the area, convened a meeting of local residents to encourage the incorporation of Jerusalem (the township that included Sugarloaf Mountain), Crocker, and Wyman townships. His argument was simple: If we're a town, we should be able to assess a lower taxation rate than the State of Maine's fifteen mils, which prevailed in all of the unorganized townships. History vindicated that argument: In 1972, after the creation of the town of Carrabassett Valley, the rate was $5 per $1,000 of valuation—just five mils.

Up on the Mountain, the Corporation built thirty-two more condominiums, all sold and ready for fall occupancy, bringing the total number of on-mountain condominiums to fifty-two. The majority of those units would be available to rent, full- or part-time, thus adding substantially to the overnight and vacation capacity right on the Mountain. Construction and sale of those units also provided an increasingly important revenue stream, as the Corporation was beginning to look as much like a real estate development enterprise as the operator of a ski area. History will show that this change of focus would carry with it some unintended consequences that would result in huge changes in the financial picture, the ultimate structure and ownership, and even the viability of the entire enterprise.

But optimism abounded in 1971, and shareholders received the following letter from President Cummings late in the summer:

*This year will be remembered as the time when Sugarloaf/USA took its place amongst the major ski areas of the world. The '71 World Cup Races combined with the first running of the Arlberg-Kandahar race outside Europe, and the attendant national television coverage, gave Sugarloaf and the State of Maine deserved international recognition as a major ski area. These events were staged and hosted by the Sugarloaf Ski Club with professional competence and the undivided support and enthusiasm of the people of the area and the State of Maine.*

*Major expansion continues this summer on the Mountain—New T-bar lift from the top of No. 3 to the summit will give full-time access to all trails and the upper lodge.*

*More grooming and seeding of trails with priority to the Narrow*

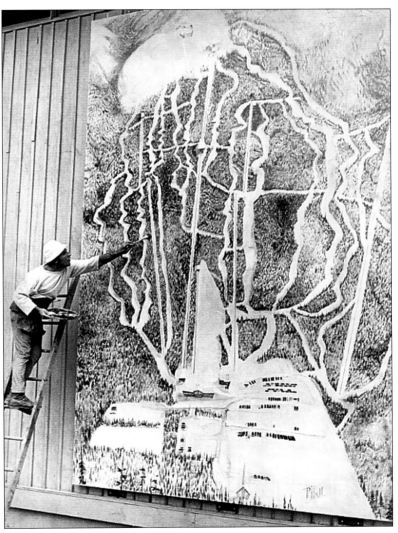

**Left:** *Parker Hall puts the finishing touches on a new trail map.*
**Right:** *On-mountain real-estate development begins.*

Gauge and Double Bitter.

A new garage is being built below the long chair. This will properly house and maintain all the vehicles necessary to continue a top-notch job of maintenance and grooming that has been so enthusiastically received during recent seasons.

Remodeling of present garage to provide an efficient and ideally located ski patrol and first-aid building.

Expansion of main lodge for increased seating area, kitchen, and food service. The lower floor is being remodeled, adding a most attractive packsack area, a new nursery, a store, and sales offices for Mountainside, our land sales and rental subsidiary.

New scenic entrance road to condominium area beginning below road to Sugarloaf Inn is complete. It adds privacy to the housing area and improves the efficiency and safety of traffic flow around the lodge.

Work on the water system, including reservoir, distribution piping, and hydrants, is going along well, and the new central sewerage system approved by the Environmental Improvement

**Above:** Welcome to the new town. **Below:** Sugarloaf trail map, 1971.

Commission earlier this year to serve the entire Mountain is progressing on schedule.

Our first year of operation of the Sugarloaf Inn met expectations and we are forecasting increased support and volume, and a break-even performance for the coming year. We are delighted that Phil Mannino and family will be returning to host the Inn again this year. Advanced bookings are coming in fast, so write or call Phil and join the crowd of Sugarloaf Inn-siders.

Sugarloaf's long-term financing was renegotiated this year and put on a far more sound basis. Jim Flint, Treasurer, ably arranged a million-dollar term loan, Maine National being the lead bank. We are most gratified with the confidence and continued broad support for Sugarloaf by the Maine banking community.

### CARRABASSETT VALLEY BECOMES A TOWN

On October 26, 1971, the residents of Jerusalem Township voted 21–13 to incorporate as Carrabassett Valley, an action that would result in

the creation of a new Maine town early the following year, with an initial town meeting to be held on April 26, 1972. The record shows that Fred Rogers of the Red Stallion cast the first vote. Crocker and Wyman townships declined to become part of the new town. (It's interesting to note that many of the local people, like Jean and Norton Luce, who lived in Crocker Township—which joined the following year—are still active in the community, and their sons and daughters are now involved in municipal affairs.)

The thirteen dissenting voters weren't necessarily opposed to the creation of a town. Many of them favored a different name—Sugarloaf, for example—but the sentiment for Carrabassett Valley as the preferred name for the new town prevailed, despite the opposition.

When the town was incorporated in 1972, the community inherited a 960-acre public lot, which up until that point had been managed by the Maine Forestry Department. Here's what I mean by *inherited*. When Maine became a state in 1820, it was divided up into townships comprised of six square miles, and within each township a so-called public lot of approximately 1,200 acres was reserved. As Maine's unsettled townships were acquired by the large timber and paper companies, agreements were reached whereby the State assumed management of the public lots. Revenues from timber management activities were paid into a fund managed by the Forestry Department, to be escrowed for the benefit of future inhabitants. In areas like Carrabassett Valley, where there was a popular demand for property on which to build camps and vacation homes, the State opened up lots to be leased by the public.

In 1971 and 1972, the *Portland Press Herald* ran a series of articles critical of the Forestry Department's management of Maine's public lots. When twenty-five people voted to create the town of Carrabassett Valley, the newspaper criticized the State for deeding the public lot to the new town. It was hypothesized that "the residents, mainly employees of the ski area, will sell the lot and use the proceeds for après-ski parties."

*The village center takes shape.*

The 1971–72 ski season, the last of the big snow years for several years to come, began auspiciously on Thanksgiving weekend and continued through May 20. Plans to operate the Gondola on the final weekend of the season were short-circuited when lightning struck the lift on Thursday, May 18. It's to be noted that a few skiers did manage to load at the mid-station for trips to the summit, unbeknownst to the Passenger Tramway Safety Board, which would have looked askance at the operation of an aerial lift whose safety system had been fried.

Total snowfall was only 46 inches less than the 246 inches that had fallen the preceding season. The downside, as mentioned previously, was that management was lulled into complacency, believing that there'd always be plenty of natural snow—so why should they invest in the equipment to manufacture the alternative? The next season showed them otherwise.

### BUSINESSES SPRING UP AND LIFTS EXPAND

Mike Gammon's ski shop, The Ski Rack in Livermore Falls, opened a store in the Valley Crossing Complex during the summer of 1972, and up on the Mountain there was a flurry of development activity. Village Center, a new on-mountain shopping and condominium complex, was constructed just west of the Base Lodge. Major space was provided for Harvey Boynton, into which he moved his ski shop. More than a few tears were shed and drafts were downed, as his old shop was demolished and, with it, Boynton's Beach. The Village Center would receive an award for design excellence from the New England Region American Institute of Architects a couple of years later at a ceremony in Worcester, Massachusetts.

On June 17, the First Annual Rangeley-Sugarloaf Golf Tournament was held at the Mingo Springs course in Rangeley. This successful event got the Sugarloaf folks to start thinking seriously about building a golf course in Carrabassett. (As an aside, I will say that the play of the Saddleback team I captained was far from inspirational!)

Al and Milu Webber built the thirty-one-unit Blue Ox Lodge near the Sugarloaf Inn, and it would be ready to accommodate 180 guests per night during the upcoming season.

Three noteworthy events occurred down in the Valley during the summer of 1972: State Route 27 was designated a scenic highway by the Maine Department of Transportation; the Dead River Company opened the Left Bank Condominiums; and there was a reported sighting of Captain America at the Sugarloaf Regional Airport.

WTOS radio began transmitting a 50,000-watt signal with a 200-mile radius from the summit. The Dead River Company proposed the construction of a dam in the Carrabassett River to create a 350-acre impoundment, but this lake was never to materialize.

In July, the Sugarloaf Mountain Corporation announced the purchase of 1,750 acres on abutting Burnt Mountain from Scott Paper Company, along with an option to purchase another 5,200 acres comprised of the easterly facing bowls on Crocker Mountain. Although the development plans for this project were intriguing, it never came to pass.

Also during that summer, Jud Strunk—who had left Sugarloaf in the mid-sixties to become a fund-raising spokesman for Bob Beattie and the U.S. Ski Team, in anticipation of the 1968 Olympics—answered the siren call of the entertainment world, picked up his banjo, went to Nashville, and thence to Hollywood, *Laugh-In,* and national tours with Andy Williams.

Leo Tague sold his Chateau des Tagues to Joe LaBeau from Orono, and his departure marked an important change in the Valley. As with the sale of so many commercial properties at so many ski areas, where the seller provides

*Sugarloaf, 1971*

part of the financing, Tague found himself the owner once again when the buyer defaulted on his loan; however, it was never quite the same.

On the evening of April 26, residents of the new town of Carrabassett Valley voted on nineteen articles in the first town warrant, at a meeting held on the second floor of the Valley Crossing Complex over Dick Ayotte's store. Patrique Mouligne was hired as Ski School director so that Harry Baxter could devote his energies full-time to management and marketing responsibilities.

### MORE LIFTS INSTALLED

During the summer of 1973, both the Double Runner East and Double Runner West chairlifts were installed on the line of the extended original T-bar, known as #2.

These lifts utilized the same towers as far as Peavey, from whence the westerly chair continued to the location of the upper terminal of the original T-bar. The longer of the two lifts, about 4,000 feet long and rising a little over 1,000 vertical feet, would load 1,200 passengers per hour—a testament to the improvement in lift technology. The eastern, shorter lift was nearly 3,100 feet long, ascending slightly more than 600 feet, and had a loading capacity similar to its westerly brother.

The 1973–74 ski season was the worst one to date, with both snow and gasoline in short supply. For the first time ever, some snow guns were borrowed to squirt some pitiful amounts of frozen white stuff in front of the Base Lodge. After the season closed, management, to show its appreciation to loyal season pass holders, sent out bumper stickers that read WE SURVIVED THE WINTER OF 1973-74.

The Sugarloaf community was saddened during the 1973–74 ski season when, on February 6, Dick Bell, sixty-six, passed away at his home in Farmington

after a valiant battle with cancer. His impact on the Mountain was, and continues to be, profound, and it's gratifying that his daughters "Buffy" and Anne, and his sister Sara's children, Brud Folger and Deanie Folger-Blake, are to this day deeply involved with Sugarloaf. They are truly carrying on Dick's legacy of devotion and commitment to the Mountain.

In the spring of 1974, Charlie Skinner was hired to oversee operations at the Mountain. Skinner had been involved in ski-area development in the Midwest, and more recently, at Squaw Mountain in Greenville (which had been purchased by Scott Paper Company).

During the summer of 1974, Skip and Eunice Skaling, who had constructed the Mountain Colony complex north on Route 27 (literally with their own hands), opened the Country Mile Restaurant in Stratton. The restaurant would be managed by their son, Steve, today a partner in the very successful Carrabassett Coffee Company.

Numerous accidental fires began taking their toll on area properties. Ed Kern's beloved Kern's Inn in Eustis, site of Jud Strunk's famous midnight ski-jumping competitions, burned in the fall, as did the Chase Bros. Warehouse in Carrabassett. These fires followed the destruction of the Stratton Diner the previous summer.

On March 13, 1974, by a vote of 24–14, the town manager form of government was adopted by the residents, and longtime Sugarloafer Preston Jordan resigned his position as first selectman to become the town's first manager.

Also during the summer of 1974, residents of Carrabassett Valley incorporated a community development firm called Western Mountains Corporation, proposing the joint planning and development of the public lots in the town of Carrabassett Valley. Dick Barringer—then director of Maine's Bureau of Public Lands and author of a book entitled *The Maine Manifest,* in which he proposed the creation of such development entities—strongly endorsed the Carrabassett initiative. His agency helped fund the development plan, and leased the state lot in what was formerly Crocker Township to the Town of Carrabassett Valley, for the development of a public ski-touring center to be operated by the Western Mountains Corporation.

The town raised $50,000 from taxation, matched the $50,000 with a federal grant from the Land and Water Conservation Fund, and borrowed $50,000

*Left: The Dead River Company's original development in Carrabassett Valley (before its move to the Sugarloaf base area.)*

from the Farmers Home Administration to build the ski-touring center and to create a trail network. This facility became a new focal point for recreational activity in the town, and held promise as an ancillary attraction to support and encourage tourism and economic development within Carrabassett Valley. More important, it made the residents of the community more confident of their ability to effect change and to initiate projects that would enhance the town's economic and social viability.

## SNOWMAKING ARRIVES

The lack of snow during the winter of 1973–74 made management on the Mountain acutely aware of the need to take steps to ensure dependable skiing. Consequently, during the summer of 1974, with some prodding from its nervous bankers, what was billed as "the world's highest snowmaking system" was installed to cover Narrow Gauge from top to bottom.

Spillway East Chairlift, some 4,020 feet long and rising nearly 1,500 vertical feet, was installed

*The famous dump party, captured in* Playboy *magazine.*

from Peavey at the top of Double Runner East to a location slightly above the unloading station of old #3 T-bar. At Hazen McMullen's insistence, the #3 T-bar, originally slated for removal, remained in place. It continues to operate dependably on windy days as the last remaining T-bar, and is still a favorite of old-time Sugarloafers. This new chair was also rated to load 1,200 passengers per hour.

Late in the summer, Harry Baxter resigned to become Paul McCollister's marketing director at the recently opened aerial tramway service at Jackson Hole, in the Tetons. Although I was sorry to see him leave Sugarloaf, I had strongly recommended Harry to Paul. I had served on the National Ski Areas Association

(NSAA) board with Paul, and I knew he had sunk a considerable fortune into his dream in Wyoming. I sensed it would be a great fit for both of them, and it was.

It was also during the summer of 1974 that there was a short-lived attempt to make Sugarloaf the "Hang Glider Capital of the East" by offering gondola rides to the summit so aficionados could ride and enjoy the ever-present thermals. This project was embarked upon, but a nervous liability insurance carrier put an end to this attempt to expand the revenue sources for the Corporation.

Real estate activity continued up and down the Valley, and on the Mountain as well, and the 1974–75 ski season saw a modest increase in skier visits to the area. As a result of all the commercial activity in the region, a sufficient supply of dependable electricity was becoming a problem. When Central Maine Power Company purchased the Rangeley Power Company in July 1975, the supply problem was solved, as CMP planned to build a new high-capacity transmission line from its generating station at Wyman Dam in Moscow.

Also in 1975, the town of Carrabassett Valley annexed Sugarloaf Township (formerly Crocker Township) as the result of legislation proposed by then senator, Neal Corson. In this transaction, however, the State of Maine retained the nearly 1,200-acre public lot.

The summer of 1975 stands out in my memory for a couple of reasons. First, I was beginning to tire of beating my head, undercapitalized as I was, against the odds of being able to make Saddleback a success. I knew it was going to require a major capital infusion to install the lifts and cut the trails to take advantage of what, to this day, is some of the most attractive skiing terrain

in the East. My presumed equity partners in such an expansion, and my land-lords, Hudson Pulp and Paper Company, decided to simultaneously sell their land and withdraw their offer to invest a cool million dollars in my project. I was tempted to keep thrashing along, praying for a miracle, until one of my

***Above left****: Modern trail groomers at work.*
***Below left:*** *Town taxes—a history.*
***Right:*** *Trail map, 1977–'78 ski season.*

investors, the sage Robert A. G. Monks, gave me some advice I've heeded in every business undertaking I've been involved with since: "You know, John, if you want to get out of a hole, the first thing you have to do is stop digging." So I did. But I was still bullish on the potential for building a true destination resort in the western mountains of Maine, and became involved with an imaginative group of developers who had a vision of a four-season village on the north side of Bigelow.

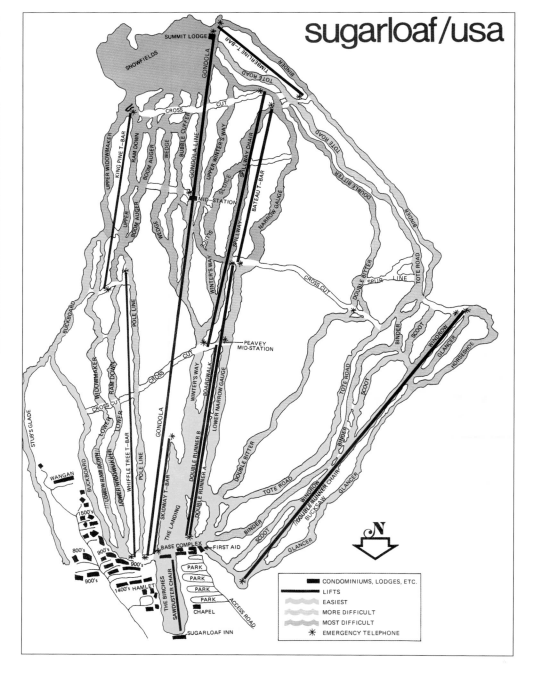

# sugarloaf/usa

Table 2

Assessed Value, Tax Rate, and Dollars Raised

1972 - 1982

| | Assessed Value | Tax Rate | Dollars Raised By Property Tax |
|---|---|---|---|
| 2 | $55,168,137 | $7.00/1000 | $386,177 |
| 1 | $42,896,247 | $7.00/1000 | $300,274 |
| 0 | $40,295,491 | $5.00/1000 | $201,477 |
| 9 * | $37,745,290 | $5.30/1000 | $200,050 |
| 8 ** | $16,045,610 | $19.50/1000 | $412,891 |
| 7 | $15,475,146 | $21.50/1000 | $332,716 |
| 6 | $14,606,596 | $19.50/1000 | $284,830 |
| 5 | $14,299,067 | $13.00/1000 | $185,888 |
| 4 | $ 6,537,390 | $8.30/1000 | $ 54,260 |
| 3 | $ 5,833,190 | $5.40/1000 | $ 31,499 |
| 2 | $ 4,927,550 | $5.00/1000 | $ 24,638 |

* Reflects revaluation of property
** State Uniform Property Tax repealed

## THE FLAGSTAFF CORPORATION AND THE BIGELOW PRESERVE

I got to know, respect, and eventually become very close friends with John Marden and John Davidson. Their Flagstaff Corporation owned 8,000 acres of land on the north side of the mountain that had spawned Sugarloaf. They had acquired this property after an earlier development initiative and enterprise had foundered.

Their vision of an "Aspen of the East," with a four-season destination village on the south shore of Flagstaff Lake, included an airport on the Stratton Flats with FAA-approved ILS (Instrument Landing System) approach angles capable of handling Boeing 727s. This plan struck me as not only bold, but quite feasible. During my years in Vermont with Walt Schoenknecht, he took me to virtually every established and emerging winter destination: Aspen, Sun Valley, Zermatt, Val d'Isère, and dozens of other locations. So I thought I had a grasp on what it took to make a ski resort work. These latter-day Bigelow Boys, it seemed to me, had the right plan. And further, I felt that their project just might be the sea swell that would lift the other boats in the harbor...namely Sugarloaf and Saddleback.

I joined the board of directors of the Flagstaff Corporation and became a modest shareholder in the enterprise. As the one "local boy" involved, I was given two tasks: first, try to get Sugarloaf's agreement that the project was in the region's best interest, and, second and even more important, try to stem the growing tide of support for an initiative launched by Lance Tapley and his deeply committed supporters who constituted an organization known as the "Friends of Bigelow." They advocated, through a petition drive and referendum vote, the creation of a state-owned recreational area to be called the Bigelow Preserve.

History tells us who was successful. I couldn't convince King Cummings that what he viewed as Sugarloaf's hegemony would not be threatened. I did convince Governor Jim Longley to be an active, visible, and staunch supporter; but I was clearly unconvincing in a series of debates with Tapley around the state. The voters, in an election that goes down in history for its low turnout, approved the creation of the Preserve.

I can, in retrospect, take some satisfaction from the result. In the first place, when the state treasury transferred several million dollars to the shareholders of the Flagstaff Corporation, we probably reaped a far-greater profit than we would ultimately have realized from a ski resort, given the traumas of the

industry over recent decades. Moreover, when I climbed the fire warden's trail on Columbus Day in 1980 and looked down on the unspoiled expanse from Avery Peak, I had been out of the ski business long enough to finally understand what had motivated Lance and his loyal legions. And I appreciated what they had done. In fact, by coincidence, in 1985, he and I had separate offices in the same building on Winthrop Street in Augusta, and I left a Bigelow Preserve map tacked to his door after what has become an annual Columbus Day ascent, with a simple, handwritten message: LANCE—THANK YOU. JOHN CHRISTIE.

## REAL ESTATE DEVELOPMENT EMBRACED

Sugarloaf's marketing efforts began to bear fruit, as during the 1975–76 ski season more than half of the Corporation's lift-related revenues were generated during the week, a clear indication that the transition was under way from a weekend ski area to a destination resort. As evidence of the Mountain's deep commitment to maximize the real estate development side of its business, Mountainside Corporation was formed on June 25, 1976, in President Cummings's words to the

shareholders, "...for the development, sales, rental, and management of real estate."

The Corporation sold the Sugarloaf Inn to Peter Webber and his wife, Martha, marking the beginning of their profound involvement in the fortunes of the entire area for years to come. The golf course and Carrabassett Valley Academy are two monuments testifying to the impact of this wonderful couple.

Bill Sim arrived as the next general manager, replacing Charlie Skinner, and the entire Valley Crossing complex and its commercial occupants were moved in pieces to the base area at the Mountain. The Red Stallion continued in operation on the Carriage Road, and a new restaurant, Tufulio's, arose on the footprint of the departed Valley Crossing structures. A new transfer station was completed on Bigelow Hill, north of Sugarloaf; this replaced the old dump, made famous in *Playboy* magazine, which had been abandoned in the early 1970s.

The Appalachian Trail was moved during the summer from Bigelow Station and off the summit of Sugarloaf to North and South Crocker peaks, crossing the Caribou Pond Road, then above the Sugarloaf cirque and joining the former trail route on the southwest side of the mountain. The trail then proceeded to the summit of Spaulding, across Oberton Stream, and thence to Saddleback. The relocation was under the direction of Steve Clark, who physically laid out the new route. (An interesting historical footnote to the story of the original Appalachian Trail on Sugarloaf: It was laid out by a local game warden, Helon Taylor, who later became the highly regarded manager of Baxter Park. One of the routes up Katahdin now bears his name.)

This relocation allowed Sugarloaf to avoid the sort of long-running battle experienced by Don Breen, who succeeded me in ownership of Saddleback. Breen would be forced to fight with the Appalachian Mountain Club and the federal government about the placement of trails, virtually paralyzing his development activities for some two decades.

By 1977, as evidence of all the development that had taken place in the Town of Carrabassett Valley since its creation in 1972, local tax revenues would grow from $24,638 to $332,716 on assessed property values of $4,927,500 and $15,475,146, respectively—and this in a town that had grown to some 200 residents, including 27 students. With the repeal of the State Uniform Property Tax in 1978, and a local revaluation in 1979, revenue from property taxes would not reach $300,000 again until 1982.

In 1978, due in part to a series of marginal snow years, and the importance of maintaining skiable surfaces, a major investment was made in state-of-the-art grooming equipment. The premier manufacturer, Kassbohrer, supplied the first of a future fleet of PistenBullies.

Sugarloafers were saddened on August 27, 1978, when word reached the Mountain that George Cary had passed away in Bath. We had all lost a great friend. When I heard the news, I was reminded that George had been such a quiet and private person; probably very few people understood or appreciated the huge contribution he had made to Sugarloaf's early growth and success. I remember saying to a mutual friend at the time that although we probably could have built the Gondola without hi, it's likely that without him, it wouldn't have been built *right!*

### LARRY WARREN NAMED PRESIDENT

In the spring of 1979, Larry Warren, who had been involved with the Corporation for over a decade with various financial management responsibilities, assumed the presidency. During that summer he negotiated the purchase of 1,170 acres of land abutting Sugarloaf's westerly boundary to accommodate future lift and trail construction, as well as residential development.

By the end of the 1970s, Sugarloaf had established itself as a true winter destination resort, with eleven ski lifts capable of transporting more than 9,000 skiers per hour. The area was, however, dependent on skiers for its revenues, and would typically be in operation less than half of each year. The Corporation board agreed that more was needed, and the upcoming decade would witness their attempt to create a genuine year-round resort.

# The Best of Times...
# The Worst of Times:
## *1980–1990*

et's begin our story about the decade of the 1980s at Sugarloaf by explaining why it should be called "the best of times...the worst of times."
On the positive side, the decade saw the realization of two important dreams, both of which are key to the current prominence of Sugarloaf. First, the vision and foresight of Peter Webber, not to mention his personal affection for the game, resulted in the construction of what is now regarded as one of the country's premier resort golf courses. And, second, his name is also linked inextricably with the other important development of the decade: the founding and early growth of a private college preparatory school to be called Carrabassett Valley Academy. It was clearly the best of times.

But up on the Mountain, despite major improvements in the uphill facilities, and seemingly rampant real estate development, dark clouds loomed over an increasingly dire financial situation. This was brought on by the combination of cost overruns in infrastructure development, and highly leveraged and expensive debt. The situation was exacerbated by discouraging results from skiing operations due to inadequate snowfall and insufficient snowmaking capacity, worsened further by customers who resisted the rising prices put in place to help support the balance sheet. Some (myself among them) would argue that a contributing factor was a major change in management focus—from ski operations to real estate and other ancillary activities—which deviated from the resort's original raison d'être.

On the one hand, steps were being taken to help enhance the area's viability as a multi-season operation with the construction of the golf course; and a school was founded that would, in the future, focus the world's attention on Sugarloaf as the womb from which many Olympic and world-class skiers and snowboarders would emerge.

*Odlin Thompson, Amos, and Stub remember the old days.*

On the other hand, some quite contrary developments were also taking place. In the offices of the Sugarloaf Mountain Corporation, management was beginning to question the viability of the enterprise under its current business model, and its ability to support itself under its increasing burden of debt. This dichotomy is the story of Sugarloaf in the 1980s.

A few miles up the road toward Canada, Stratton Lumber, organized in 1979, began operations in May 1981, drastically changing the economics of the town of Eustis. The timing couldn't have been better for the small community, as Forster Mfg. Co. was, that same year, closing its wood-turning manufacturing plant.

The 1980s began with a flurry of base area activity, with the addition of Village South, a hotel/condominium complex with three commercial properties; the Corporation's acquisition of Harvey Boynton's Ski Shop (Harvey having passed away in 1976 at the age of fifty-five); and the construction of Gondola Village just below the lower terminal of the Gondola, to include a modern nursery facility and specially designed meeting and conference rooms.

*"THE STREAK"*

A very important milestone was marked in 1981, as over the years that followed, skiers and non-skiers alike, both in- and outside of Maine, would follow with growing interest what would become known as "The Streak." The fully clothed streaker was one Paul Schipper, and let's listen to part of his story as he told it in 1999, in the Sugarloaf Mountain Ski Club's 50th Anniversary Magazine:

*It was an early day in May 1981 when three of my ski buddies, my*

*dog "Mogul," and I hiked up to the summit of Sugarloaf Mountain for one last run. As I recall it was a nice sunny day— blue sky and tons of snow on the trails—yet the Mountain was officially closed. We rested in the sun at the "Gondi" building, had a beer and sandwich, and tried to make the big decision on which trail was the best and most rewarding for our descent. During our conversation, the number of days we'd skied that year came up. We realized that by coincidence, all four of us had skied almost every day the Mountain had been open that year. In every case, the few days missed were for the most part trivial reasons. Anyway, then and there we all resolved that the next season, we'd ski every single day the Mountain was*

**Above:** *Paul Schipper*

*open. That was how the Streak started!*

*Using that year as a start, I had skied the last 135 consecutive days of the season. I haven't missed a day the Mountain has been open since. This year, May 2, 1999, the number is 177 days, and the Streak now totals 3,077 days.*

It wouldn't be until 2005 that the Streak would finally come to an end. By that time, Paul had his own private parking space at the base of the lifts, a world-wide reputation for his tenacity, and a place in the hearts of all Sugarloafers.

The summer of 1981 saw the snowmaking system double in size to cover 110 acres; Al Webber sold his Blue Ox Inn to Peter Webber, who renamed it Timberwind; and the University of Maine, which owned the Capricorn Lodge (thanks to the generosity of Maine philanthropist Harold Alfond), sold the building to Raye Baumind. Alfond had been introduced to the Sugarloaf area by his good friend Bob Marden, a former president of the Maine state Senate, a Sugarloaf director, and a prominent Waterville attorney. He had become convinced of the importance to the state of the continued development of the area, and his investment in the Capricorn was evidence of that.

On October 5, 1981, Sugarloafers and millions of people nationwide were saddened when our adopted "favorite son," Jud Strunk, died in a plane crash. A private pilot, Jud suffered a heart attack shortly after takeoff from the Sugarloaf Regional Airport; the plane crashed, killing Jud and another Sugarloaf stalwart, Dick Ayotte. Jud was only forty-five.

I can't overstate the impact Jud had on my life. His ability to capture the essence of what Maine is all about and to retell our stories in an unforgettable way has never been equaled. Everyone adored Jud, and, through him, they also fell in love with Maine. As S.J. Perelman would have said, Before they made Jud Strunk, they threw away the mold!

The growth of commercial and residential development in the area was beginning to impose significant environmental impacts, the most significant being discharged wastewater. The Class A Watershed designation of the environs of the Carrabassett River required the development of improved water-treatment facilities. In 1982, Sugarloaf formed a nonprofit subsidiary, Sugartech, to own and operate sewer lines and a wastewater-treatment facility. Industrial revenue bonds were authorized in the amount of $2,500,000 to undertake construction. This 11.5 percent tax-exempt debt issue funded the construction of a "slow-rate spray irrigation" treatment plant on the westerly border of the town near the Wyman town line. The plant pioneered a water storage system that fed a snowmaking system in the winter months. This resulted in a mountain of man-made snow on Bigelow Hill each year that nobody wanted to ski. The facility and its network of sewer lines would assure capacity for further development and meet the stringent environmental requirements inherent in a Class A Watershed.

### AMOS WINTER PASSES AWAY

On January 5, 1982, Amos Winter passed away at the age of eighty. Everyone even remotely connected to Sugarloaf, and people from all over who had only heard about this remarkable man, were deeply saddened. My good friend David

*Paul Schipper*

Rowan, publisher of *Ski Area Management* magazine, asked me if I'd write a little something as a tribute in his February issue:

*Once, years ago, I overheard a skier at Sugarloaf who had the misfortune to get a traffic ticket on his way to the mountain ask Amos what kind of treatment he might expect from Judge Benoit, before whom he was scheduled to appear the following morning in Farmington.*

*"Well," said Amos, "let me put it this way. If I ordered a boxcar full of sons of bitches and all they sent was Judge Benoit, I wouldn't feel cheated."*

*There's a whole generation of us whose years in the ski business were influenced by this unusual man, and we could safely say that if we ordered a boxcar full of the people who had a lasting effect on us, both professionally and personally, and all they sent was Amos Winter, we wouldn't feel cheated.*

**Left:** *Jud Strunk.* **Right:** *Amos*

*For a man who achieved so much, it's a paradox that those of us who loved him will remember him least for his achievements.*

*We'll forget that he literally, and at times almost single-handedly, created the ski industry in Maine as we now know it; we'll forget that it was Amos, and Bill Whitney and others of that unique breed, who gave birth to the organizations that now serve the industry so effectively; and we'll probably even forget that it was Amos who had the vision that has given us the Sugarloaf of today . . . and even tomorrow.*

*We'll forget all those things because he'll live with us for what he* **was**, *not for what he did.*

*He was a good man.*

*He was so honest that some of us who were seizing every opportunity to promote this growing sport some twenty years ago were driven to distraction by his truthfulness. But every one of us who learned that, and many other lessons at his knee, have conducted our lives a little differently because of his example.*

*He was a generous man.*

*Under that sometimes gruff exterior was a man who gave so willingly of his time and boundless energy that he sometimes seemed to live for the exclusive purpose of helping other people.*

*He was my friend.*

*He tried to teach me everything he knew...not just about the business we were in together, but about what I could expect from the world, and should expect from myself. He taught me never to be disappointed with what the former had to offer, and never be satisfied with what the latter accomplished.*

*During the past twenty years, as I look back, a surprising number of the decisions I've made have been preceded by a question I've asked myself: "What would Amos think?"*

*I suspect there are a lot of people whose lives he touched who subconsciously ask themselves that same question.*

*Our decisions are better ones for having asked it.*

*And since I plan to continue asking that same question for the rest of my life, Amos Winter, for me, is still very much alive.*

## PETER WEBBER AND THE SUGARLOAF GOLF COURSE

In August 1982, the Bigelow Corporation sold its remaining property in what had formerly been Crocker Township to Peter Webber. On October 6, Peter conveyed to the Town of Carrabassett Valley land enough to accommodate a golf course. An agreement was signed between Sugarloaf Mountain Corporation, Peter N. Webber Enterprises, the Town of Carrabassett Valley, and Robert Trent Jones Jr. for the design and construction of a "championship golf course." Mountain Greenery, a joint venture between Peter N. Webber and Sugarloaf Mountain Corporation, then proceeded to develop 1,600 acres of land.

Construction of the golf course was well under way, and roads and utility lines were constructed in adjacent areas to form the beginnings of a new real estate development to be called Village on the Green. Eight Bigelow condominium units were constructed, and the new wastewater treatment facility on Bigelow Hill was brought on line.

In 1983, Spillway East and Double Runner East and West chairlifts were rebuilt, and Spillway West, with a vertical rise of more than 1,000 feet, was installed. All the T-bars received major overhauls, as they were all more than twenty years old.

## THE TOWN STEPS IN

It was clear that the construction and operation of the golf course would require some creative financing. Fortunately, the voters of the Town of Carrabassett Valley were willing to go along with the arrangement. Here's how it worked: The Town put up $1 million. It took $250,000 from its reserve fund and borrowed $750,000

## The Gondola Is Retired

The emerging technology of detachable four-passenger chairs capable of transporting four times as many passengers per hour. And at its worst, the gondola was unable to operate on many days when the wind would have no deleterious effect on a chairlift. And finally, The Mighty Gondola, like a tired racehorse, was just beginning to wear out, and replacement parts were becoming harder and harder to find. She had done the job assigned to her: get people to Sugarloaf. But the time had come to find better ways to transport skiers up the Mountain once they got there. And the original vision of scores of summer and autumn passengers had just never materialized.

To provide skiers continuing access to the snowfields, a T-bar was installed west of Tote Road. The diesel engine powering the #6 T-bar could be heard far and wide, but it enabled the faithful to get to the highest reaches of the Mountain.

The following year, a fabulous fundraiser was held in the Base Lodge—a festive Gondola Auction, where a dozen gondola cabins were auctioned for the benefit of local charities. My heart was especially warmed when one of Jud Strunk's sons, Rory, became the proud owner of one of them. I'm sure Jud was smiling down on that event!

Today, the old lower terminal (the one I had located in the brook) houses the Sugarloaf Competition Center, the headquarters for all competitions held on the Mountain, as well as the offices and archives of the Sugarloaf Mountain Ski Club.

by issuing municipal bonds. Sugarloaf put up $1 million through a limited real estate partnership. The partnership would be reimbursed by having the real estate taxes waived for the period of the arrangement. In addition, the partnership would receive two-thirds of the municipal bond principal payments.

The lease included an option for Sugarloaf to extend the lease for a $2,500 annual payment, subject to adjustment for inflation. The anticipated benefit from the golf course for the town and Sugarloaf was the development of a summer focus for property owners, enhancement of the potential for real estate sales and development of the town, and increased employment and business opportunities for the residents and businesses of the community. There was little expectation of profitability in the operation of the golf course at the outset of the plan. Sugarloaf, in fact, anticipated a $25,000 to $50,000 annual subsidy of the golf operations from real estate and skiing operations.

## CARRABASSETT VALLEY ACADEMY

While these developments were taking place, an educational dream was being realized. Back in 1969, the Sugarloaf Regional Ski Educational Foundation (SRSEF) was created to help racers and freestyle skiers sharpen their competitive skills. Members of the Foundation had been dreaming of the day they could establish a genuine ski academy that would accommodate young athletes who wanted to combine their interest in competitive skiing with a superior college preparatory education close to home in the western mountains. The dream was realized during the 1982–83 academic year when, with fifteen initial students, Carrabassett Valley Academy opened its doors, with classes held in the Dick Bell Chapel. Without a permanent home until the following

year, when operations would be consolidated in the former Capricorn Lodge, it was clear from the beginning that King Cummings's visionary impetus, along with that of a handful of other pioneers, would form the foundation for an educational and athletic success story. Cummings was the single most important

the academy co-own and operate the complex. Usage is based on initial and ongoing funding. CVA has use of the facility 35% of the time. The town has use the remaining 65% and facilitates programs during its public hours. A major fundraising initiative was undertaken to generate the capital necessary to con-

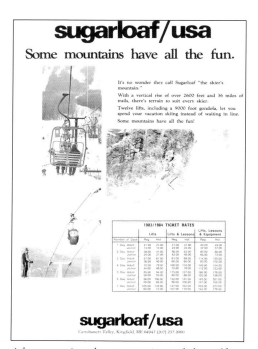

John Ritzo, CVA headmaster.

Ads promoting the mountain and the golf course.

contributor, not only to Sugarloaf's survival during its traumatic teenage years, but also as the one far-sighted thinker whose vision included more than just the development of a ski area. CVA added a significant new dimension to the Sugarloaf community.

By 1991, under the leadership of John Ritzo, who had been appointed headmaster in 1986, the school would be accredited by the New England Association of Schools and Colleges. In 1996, the school purchased the Lumberjack Lodge, which now houses its female students. In 2001, the Anti-Gravity Recreation Complex—a world-class training center for CVA—was constructed as a joint venture between the town and the academy. The town and

struct a campus removed from busy Route 27. With an annual operating budget in excess of $3,000,000, and a payroll of more than $1,300,000, CVA is today the area's second-largest employer, with more than 40 year-round employees, and 120 students enrolled annually.

Over its first quarter century, CVA has become recognized as a leader among snow sports academies throughout the world. It has produced ten Olympians (one Olympic gold medal, two silver medals, one bronze medal), six world champions, and fifteen NCAA All-Americans. Graduates have also claimed one Overall Alpine World Cup title, two Individual Alpine World Cup titles, and seventy National Championship titles. Everyone in Maine knows the names of

Bode Miller and Seth Wescott and Kirsten Clark, and the ski world recognizes and reveres dozens more.

CVA is in the process of building a new facility that will add to the Valley's world-class inventory of attractions. This state-of-the-art residential dormitory will further enhance the recruiting capacity of the school.

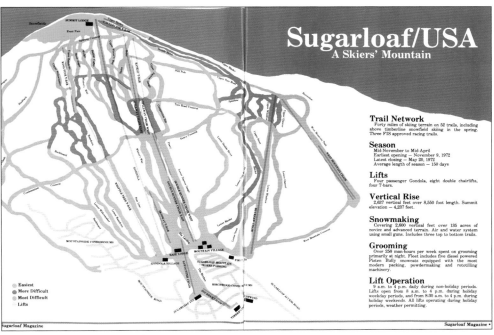

*Sugarloaf, 1984, showing the expansion to West Mountain.*

### WEST MOUNTAIN DEVELOPED

In 1984, three new trails were cut on the upper part of the mountain, and a nearly 7,000-foot double chairlift, West Mountain, was installed, running from the golf course area to the top of Bucksaw Chair, ascending nearly 1,300 vertical feet with an intermediate loading and unloading station about two-thirds of the way up. The lower terminal would serve double duty as the clubhouse for the course. Work continued on the golf course with fairway seeding and the installation of

a water collector and pump house in the Carrabassett River, to provide not only irrigation for the course, but also additional water for expanded snowmaking.

Base Lodge expansion continued with the construction of a new west wing to provide expanded skier services, including ski rentals, a 180-seat restaurant, a coffee shop, and a 300-seat lounge. A separate office building was constructed to house the Corporation's sales and administrative activities, and condominium construction included seventeen Bigelow units in the Mountainside development, and sixteen at Village on the Green.

Also during the summer of 1984, the Snubber chairlift, 5,425 feet in length, was installed to carry residents of properties below the Sugarloaf Inn to the base area and to provide access for skiers utilizing a parking lot near its lower terminal.

In 1985, the eagerly anticipated opening of the Sugarloaf Golf Course took place. That same year, work began on the 102-unit Sugarloaf Hotel, just west of the Base Lodge. Built at a cost of some $8,500,000, the facility would contain meeting rooms and more than 3,000 square feet of commercial space. While the hotel would definitely add to Sugarloaf's appeal as a year-round destination resort, it would prove to be at a very substantial and ulti-mately survival-threatening cost.

Two new trails were cut in an area east of #5 T-bar, in an area to be named King Pine, opening up some new, very challenging terrain.

*BANKRUPTCY*

The frenetic pace of development during the mid-1980s was catching up with the Corporation's ability to sustain—or even manage—it. Revenues from the various available streams proved to be insufficient to meet creditor and lender demands, and the debt burden was simply too large for the operation to sup-port. On March 23, 1986, under pressure from its creditors and in the final con-struction throes of the excessively expensive Sugarloaf Hotel, the Sugarloaf Mountain Corporation filed a petition for protection under the provisions of Chapter 11 of the United States Bankruptcy Code. King Cummings assumed the reins as chief executive officer, and a cloud obscured the bright sun that had been shining on the Mountain.

I'm reminded of a comment made by Jake Barnes, the tragic hero in Ernest Hemingway's *The Sun Also Rises,* when he was asked how he had gone bankrupt.

"Two ways," he said. "Very slowly, and suddenly." Anyone who has gone through it knows what Jake meant. The fact is, although it does take time to get into a position where there's no other way out, the final act is swift and dramatic.

Once under the protection of the court, the Mountain proceeded to

***Right and above:*** *The Sugarloaf Hotel.*

undertake necessary summer maintenance and to even complete the installation of an expanded and more efficient snowmaking system at a cost of about $2,000,000. It increased coverage of skiable terrain from 38 percent to 55 percent, and included top-to-bottom coverage on West Mountain Chairlift Line, Bucksaw Chairlift Line, and Competition Hill. Three new compressors were added, capable of producing 3,000 cubic feet of air per minute and the capacity to operate sixty-five snow guns.

In July 1986, Larry Warren resigned as president of both Sugarloaf Mountain Corporation and Mountainside. On November 3, Warren Cook was named president of Sugarloaf Mountain Corporation, and on December 19, assumed the same position with Mountainside. Jerry Muth, who had arrived in August from Colorado, was named vice president and general manager of Sugarloaf Mountain Corporation, and on December 19 was named executive

vice president and chief operating officer of Mountainside.

On August 1, the Mountain had sold two condominium projects that were under way to the Dartmouth Company, which took over all of Mountainside's real estate marketing and sales activities. Additionally, the Corporation entered into an agreement with Boston Conces-sions Group for the operation of all food and beverage sales on the Mountain.

In 1987, Sugarloaf continued to operate under the protection of the court as it attempted to reorganize its operations, and on April 3 the bankruptcy court approved a joint plan of reorganization for Sugarloaf and its wholly owned subsidiary, Mountainside. This included an infusion of new capital, raised in large part through the extraordinary efforts of King Cummings.

President Cook, in a letter to shareholders dated April 17, 1986, revealed the reorganization plan approved by the court, which, in its simplest translation, advised the owners of the company that they must choose to accept either one of two alternative plans: one provided for the exchange of their shares for shareholder credits toward the purchase of lift tickets during either the 1988–89 ski season; and the other, for the five ski seasons commencing with that season. (Nobody ever said holders of common stock make out well in a bankruptcy.)

Despite the dark cloud of bankruptcy, indomitable Sugarloaf skiers continued to enjoy and promote their chosen mountain. During the 1986–87 ski season, the lifts ran, snow was made, parties were held, and life for the skiers didn't markedly change. One noteworthy occurrence was a minor accident in the lower terminal of the Gondola that provided clear evidence the device might be nearing the end of its productive life.

Another visible dampener was the Five-Hundred-Year Flood on April 1 that demonstrated what Mother Nature was capable of doing when she really wanted to put a damper on things. Torrential rains washed away entire sections of the "S" turns on Route 27, along with Ken Packard's bridge across the Carrabassett to Ted Jones's house and the Clay Brook Bridge farther down the road. The great slide now evident on the west side of Crocker Mountain was reportedly attributed to the deluge, and the Golf Course received considerable damage, which resulted in the reconstruction of portions of the course.

In 1987, up in Stratton, a 30-megawatt, wood-burning, electricity-generating plant began operation, as did the Western Maine Children's Museum down in the Valley. (The museum's name would be changed to the Western Maine Center for Children in 2001.)

## SNOWMAKING AND HIGH-CAPACITY QUADS

In the summer of 1988, three new lifts were built, 110 new acres of skiing terrain opened, two state-of-the-art groomers were added to the fleet, fifty additional snowmaking guns were purchased, and the snowmaking air and water

*Sugarloaf, 1988*

systems were expanded. This marked the first major focus on improving the skiing experience under President Cook, and recognition that if the Mountain were to ultimately thrive, it was the return to the culture of a real skiers' mountain that would provide the answer. This was a remarkable set of developments so soon after the bankruptcy filing. And there was more to come.

More than a million and a half dollars were spent on two four-passenger chairlifts, each capable of loading 2,400 passengers per hour. One of these quads would carry skiers up over the previously cut Haulback trail, which descended from the top of #5 T-bar into the basin east of Upper Widowmaker. A new trail called Choker was cut that also returned to the base of the quad. These black diamond trails would not only provide skiing on another piece of terrain, but the northeasterly exposure would also provide an opportunity for skiers to get out of the wind and to enjoy the faint morning rays of the midwinter sun.

The other quad replaced and ascended somewhat higher than the old #4 T-bar. From the top, skiers could descend to the bottom of the Haulback lift, go down Lower Ramdown, Lower Widowmaker, or Buckboard to the base, or continue on up to the top on T-bar #5 on days when it was appropriate to operate that lift.

A third chairlift, a two-seater, was installed to replace the Skidway T-bar that serviced the expansive beginners' area (called The Landing) in front of the Base Lodge. In announcing these developments, Sugarloaf's director of operations, former instructor and coach John Diller, noted that the Mountain's fourteen lifts would have a total uphill capacity of more than 17,000 skiers per hour—a full 40 percent increase over the previous year.

"We recognized our inability to get people up the hill," he noted in a letter to Sugarloafers. "We had lift lines last year, but our commitment is very strong to keep the lift lines down this year. That is why we are adding the lifts."

Upper Widowmaker was nearly doubled in width, from 90 to 175 feet,

*King Cummings.*

and Haulback was turned into a 299-foot-wide slope for what the Mountain would refer to in its promotional materials as "uncrowded cruising." Two new groomers, PistenBully Winch Cats, together costing about a quarter of a million dollars, expanded the fleet to seven, and front-mounted winches permitted the machines to groom even the steepest pitches.

The entire Sugarloaf community—indeed, the whole state of Maine—was saddened during the 1988–89 ski season when King Cummings was suddenly taken ill in March and died shortly thereafter. Next to Amos Winter, King was the single person most responsible for the emergence of Sugarloaf as a major player in the world of skiing. In its worst of times, King stepped up and nearly single-handedly engineered its emergence from bankruptcy. Jean Luce, in a tribute to him in the Sugarloaf Ski Club Magazine, stated it well: "He was always in on the ground floor of getting a project off and running...the Chapel, the Ski Foundation, the World Cup, Carrabassett Valley Academy...not always tangible; in fact, usually in subtle ways. We have lost a great friend."

The 1989–90 ski season saw the successful organization and execution of one of the largest racing events held at the Mountain up to that time: the Michelob Light Masters National Championship. The weeklong event proved that Sugarloaf was capable of hosting competitions of almost any scale. Additionally, the U.S. Ski Team had utilized the Mountain as its early-season training site, and made plans to do so again the following year.

The turbulent decade of the '80s saw Sugarloaf persevere through its trials and flourish with its successes. Through it all, its loyal supporters, both skiers and investors, remained faithful to its indomitable spirit. The employees, even in the worst of times, embodied the outgoing friendliness and hospitality that had become a hallmark of the Mountain.

# Growth and Transition
## *1990–2000*

**5**

The bankruptcy during the preceding decade caused ripples that brought real estate activity in the early 1990s to a virtual standstill, as potential property owners waited to see what the future might hold. The Corporation routinely reorganized its financial and equity structure with the assistance of various interested individuals, and even faced the prospect in the early part of the decade of another bankruptcy filing. It wasn't until 1993 that the situation would begin to stabilize with the sale of some assets and the infusion of new capital.

Finances aside, Sugarloaf continued to be the destination of choice for a faithful cadre of recreational skiers, and a preferred competition site for the racing community. In 1993 the Sugarloaf Competition Department was formed, assuming what had historically been the responsibility of the Sugarloaf Mountain Ski Club. It would function as a department of the Mountain, to be assisted by the Ski Club and Carrabassett Valley Academy. This level of organization, and the Mountain's reputation as a premier competition venue, resulted in a nearly mind-boggling succession of races held during the 1990s: U.S. Snowboard Championships, U.S. Chevy Trucks Alpine National Championships, U.S. Snowboard Grand Prix, U.S. Chevy Trucks Freestyle National Championships, U.S. Masters Alpine Championships, North American Junior Alpine Championships, and the Eastern Junior Olympics.

As a result of its now well-established reputation for conducting first-class competitions, Sugarloaf was twice awarded the prestigious Paul Bacon Award by the United States Ski Association.

*SNOWBOARDING ARRIVES*

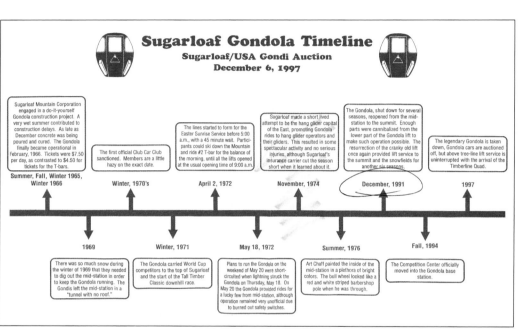

It was also during the '90s that snowboarding was beginning to take its place alongside skiing. An argument can be made that without the advent of this new sport and its attraction for a whole new generation, ski areas in general—and Sugarloaf in particular—would have faced even tougher, perhaps devastating, financial times. Sugarloaf welcomed snowboarders, and in response to their need for somewhat nontraditional terrain, half-pipes and terrain parks were specifically designed and constructed for their use.

Even while traditionalists and purists fueled the debate about whether skiing and snowboarding were even compatible, management recognized the economic reality and embraced this growing new clientele.

*THE TOWN COMES TO THE RESCUE*

In the fall of 1992, Warren Cook and his management team turned to the Town of Carrabassett Valley to assist them in the development of a financial plan to enable Sugarloaf to continue as a viable operation. The town purchased Sugarloaf's wastewater treatment facilities for $3 million, created the Carrabassett Valley Sanitary District, and issued $3.7 million in general obligation bonds of the town to provide badly needed mortgage financing for the Mountain. A half million dollars of the town's recreation reserve funds was pledged in escrow as debt-service reserve funds for the new bonds. The Finance Authority of Maine's loan guarantees that were in place on already-existing Corporation debt were redirected at securing another $2 million in working capital loans. In return for the implementation of the town's refinancing plan, Fleet Bank wrote off some $1.7 million of the debt it held, which further helped to stabilize the Corporation's finances. In return for its support, the town included as a provision of its financing a requirement that Sugarloaf would pay a $600,000 fee on final repayment of the bonds.

## THE S-K-I ERA

The result of this reorganization of Sugarloaf's debt was twofold. First, it allowed operations to continue; and second, it encouraged investment in the enterprise

by S-K-I Ltd., an outside entity experienced in ski-area operation. This provided at least a short-term answer to the needs of the area, and led to major upgrades and improvements in the ski operation.

Preston Leete Smith, whom I got to know well during my days at Mount Snow, and who sat with me on the boards of both the Vermont and National Ski Area Associations, was a sort of latter-day Walter Schoenknecht. A little less of a visionary and a lot more of a businessman than Walt, Pres had attended public schools in West Hartford, Connecticut, prep school at Oakwood in Poughkeepsie, New York, and earned a Bachelor of Science degree from Earlham College in Richmond, Indiana. His daughter Leslie had been on the U.S. Ski Team from 1975–80, and was on the 1976 and 1980 Olympic Teams. He had assembled what was the first ski-area conglomerate, which by 1994 included Killington, Mount Snow, and Haystack in Vermont; Waterville Valley in New Hampshire; and Bear Valley in California.

*Snowboarding arrives to help save skiing.*

He was one of a new breed of ski-resort developers who didn't enter the business as a lifelong devotee, an expert skier, or an alumnus of the famed Tenth Mountain Division. Or, like myself and many of my contemporaries, via the "ski bum" route. He was more focused on the "business" of skiing. He understood better than many of us who were building and operating ski areas at the time what it would take to interest people in the sport, and how to get novices and intermediates to the hill: dependable, high-quality skiing on carefully groomed terrain with lots of man-made snow; easily accessible and inexpensive instruction on skis the length of which would be determined by the skier's ability; a guarantee that after a week of instruction, one would be able to call oneself a skier; and plenty of fast, comfortable, uphill transportation.

When he arrived with $2 million in hand and an offer to invest it in return for a 51 percent controlling interest in the enterprise, both Sugarloaf and the town recognized the offer was too good to refuse. And from the skiers' standpoint, it was a gift from heaven, because the following year, a new signature lift—a high-speed detachable quad called the "Super Quad"—was installed. The Super Quad extended from the base area to a shoulder above the Rock Garden on Tote Road, and would give access to not only Narrow Gauge above the Headwall and all the trails to the east, but also to Competition Hill and all the terrain between it and Double Bitter. New trails Hayburner and King's Landing (named for King Cummings) were developed, creating arguably the most popular terrain on the Mountain for latter-day Sugarloafers.

## ENTER LES OTTEN

In 1996, Pres Smith's protégé, Les Otten, assembled a mega-enterprise the likes of which American skiing had never seen. Otten had worked for Pres Smith at Killington, and had gone to Sunday River to operate it for (and then buy it from) him. By 1996, Otten had grown his business sufficiently to purchase S-K-I Ltd. from Pres Smith. He named his new enterprise, appropriately, the American Skiing Company. The ski world awoke one day and tried to digest the news that S-K-I Ltd. had been sold to Les Otten and his emerging company.

In what now seems like the blink of an eye, Otten's company grew to include Killington, Mount Snow, Haystack, and Sugarbush in Vermont; Attitash, Cranmore, and Waterville Valley in New Hampshire; Sunday River and Sugarloaf in Maine; Heavenly Valley in California; Steamboat in Colorado; The Canyons (formerly Park City West) in Utah; and a golf course in Florida. Waterville Valley and Cranmore were sold shortly after the conglomerate was assembled for antitrust reasons, and the golf course was unloaded to generate needed cash.

For a while, it looked like Les Otten was the genius the ski world had been waiting for—but it needs to be noted that virtually every property in his portfolio was suffering from balance sheet problems similar to Sugarloaf's, to one degree or another. This was due to a flattening in the growth of new entrants to the sport, some bad snow years, and skyrocketing costs of utilities, insurance,

equipment, and labor. Testimony to the tough times was the fact that even the best-conceived and -managed resorts in the country had run out their credit, and credibility, with their banks. (The premier example of this in my mind was Waterville Valley in New Hampshire, developed by my good friend Tom Corcoran.)

### Wait 'til you see
# What's New at Sugarloaf

# SuperQuad™ will make the difference

*Sugarloaf's Multi-year Development Plan Begins With An Uphill Capacity Increase of 35%*

This winter Sugarloaf skiers will enjoy the ride on the fastest high-speed detachable quad in the world. The new Sugarloaf SuperQuad™ will benefit skiers with its sheer speed and length, covering more miles and variety of terrain than any single lift in New England, all in a matter of six short minutes! This state-of-the-art four-passenger chair is an impressive lift, covering 7,000 feet and rising 1,800 vertical feet out of the Sugarloaf Village. It is powered by more horsepower than any other chairlift in the East, a total of 900 h.p.! The lift increases

the mountain's uphill capacity by approximately 35 percent. It is a high-tech machine, but that's not where the excitement ends. what really excites skiers is the terrain the SuperQuad™ will serve.

### Lots more ski-time in store

New for 1994/95 is 60 acres of blue square and single black diamond terrain located right in the heart of the SuperQuad™ pod! The new terrain, of course, will have full snowmaking capacity installed, and be open for skiing early in the season. Options for

intermediate skiers are extensive and very long. Blue square trails off the new lift are all over two miles in length, including favorites like Tote Road, Double Bitter, Haywire, Chaser and King's Landing, plus all the trails in the Bucksaw area. Intermediates will love skiing the SuperQuad™ because of the time they'll spend going downhill on a variety of terrain. Experts have their choice of the East's steepest mogul run, Skidder, or carving turns on the steep groomed fall-lines of trails like Narrow Gauge, Competition Hill, or the new superhighway,

Hayburner. The SuperQuad™ is the fastest chairlift available in the world, so skiers better be in shape because this means spending lots of fun time on skis.

### More 'boarding, bedding & libation

In addition, the snowboard park has been doubled in size to seven acres, and a second snowboarding half-pipe will be added that meets ISF and USSA specifications. Twelve new condo units bring on-mountain lodging capacity from 7,000 to 7,100 people. A microbrewery and new restaurant

in the Sugarloaf Village round out this summer's improvements.

This summer's expansions are part of a multi-year development plan which will see Maine's largest ski mountain expand skiable terrain, snowmaking capacity, lift capacity and on-mountain village over the next five years. The expansion was made possible by an agreement with a new equity partner, S-K-I, Ltd., of Killington, Vermont. Daily management of the resort will remain in the hands of owner Warren Cook. Sugarloaf/USA is Maine's largest four-season resort and conference center.

*Compiled U.S.A. News Bureau*

**Left:** *The Superquad arrives.* **Right:** *l–r: Warren Cook honors Stub Taylor on his retirement in 1996.*

In an unfortunate coincidence, this was also a time when prestigious banks like the institution financing Waterville Valley, The First of Boston, were having grave problems as well by overextending credit to real estate developers.

So the dominoes were starting to fall, and lots of ski-area investors and creditors were looking for a savior. Enter Les Otten with his vision and charisma. Soon, folks were flocking to him, eager to hear his plans for salvation. Otten was good for Sugarloaf and the Town of Carrabassett Valley at the time. When American Skiing bought S-K-I Ltd.'s 51 percent interest in the Mountain, followed shortly thereafter by its acquisition of the remaining 49 percent, the result was the repayment of the bonds issued by the town on Sugarloaf's behalf in 1993; the collection of the $600,000 financing fee; and relief of

the town's requirement to maintain a $500,000 debt-service reserve fund for the bonds. The newly injected funds, net of prepayment penalty fees associated with the financing, were deposited in a reserve account of the Town—a town which, by this time, claimed a population of some 349 people.

My return to the mountain I had left almost thirty years before coincided with American Skiing's acquisition, and I was struck by the fact that Sugarloaf seemed both so different from what it had been in 1968, and yet so much the same. The difference lay in the layout and the facilities, and the sheer scale of the development. Case in point: My return was provoked by "Chip" Carey's invitation to play a role in a festive retirement party for Stub Taylor, to be held in the spring of 1996. Since my sons had recently gotten me back on alpine skis, I was ready to spend some time at the Mountain. I had just finished up some work I had been doing for Bangor Savings Bank and hadn't determined exactly what my next business venture might be, so the month of March was open. I felt it was appropriate that I spend as much of it at Sugarloaf as possible. Warren Cook, in his generosity, wanted to give me a season pass for the balance of the season, saying, "Take this note to Guest Services and they'll take your picture and give you a pass."

I was too proud to ask the obvious question: "Where the hell is Guest Services?" Assuming it must be in the Base Lodge, I headed in that direction. Along the way, I ran into an old Sugarloafer and buddy from Bangor, Ted Sherwood. When I asked him where I should go, he said, "I think Guest Services is about where your old apartment used to be." It was; nonetheless, I was pleased when Ted kindly agreed to give me a guided tour of the entire mountain.

Although the sheer expanse of the layout and the quality of the skiing were quite different from what I had known almost thirty years before, the people were the same. After just one day back, it felt like I had never left. And it's not just that the folks reminded me of the people I had loved and skied and partied with in the 1960s; they were the same people, and they were all around: Bill Jones, Bill Haefle, Brud Folger, Buffy and Annie Bell, Dan Davis, Bruce Miles, John Diller, and Henry Bacon...I could go on and on. And even Dennis Parsons, whom I had hired on the recommendation of his uncle, "Stub" Taylor, to run the #4 T-bar in 1963, was still there—and still running a lift. John Chapman and Herb Hoefler's wife Liz were still down in Campbell Field. Don Fowler was on Poplar Stream, and Neal Trask, Al Webster, and all my old neighbors were still in their camps in Spring Farm. Rand Stowell's son, Randy, was still in the family condo-

*"Mr. Sugarloaf" and Maine Ski Hall of Famer, Stub Taylor*

minium up off Buckboard, and Greg Foster was spending every weekend at his place down in Sugarloaf Village.

It seemed like hardly anything had changed. And the Sugarloaf spirit had not only survived...it had flourished!

Alongside these old friends from Sugarloaf's past was a whole new group of Sugarloafers who I could see shared the same love and devotion for the Mountain. The only difference: Whereas we had built camps on the Carrabassett for $2,500, they were now buying condominiums for $250,000. I knew after a few days why I was glad to be home, and, more important, that whatever had happened or might happen in the future, the place was going to survive. Too many people felt too strongly about the Mountain to accept anything less.

Enough sentimentality. Let's get back to the story. In 1996, following American Skiing's acquisition, a second high-speed detachable quad was installed to replace the fixed-grip Whiffletree Quad, which was moved, in part, to the westerly shoulder of the mountain, terminating near the summit. Its terminal, dubbed Timberline, was near the unloading area of the diesel-driven #6 T-bar, which had been taken out of service in 1975. This lift once again allowed skiers to gain access to the summit and the snowfields, as well as the diamond and double-diamond trails on the face of the Mountain. It also opened up cruising on new trails beneath and to the west of the chair.

In 1997, American Skiing went public with an initial public offering in November at $18 per share. It looked like Les Otten was one guy who had figured out how to make money in the ski business. But in many important ways, the ski business is like any other—its principal goal is to stay in business. Many things can get in the way of this objective: when you try to grow too fast; when you start to believe your own glowing press releases about yourself; when you take your eye off the ball; when events and phenomena over which you have no control (like the weather, the price of oil, and the economy) conspire against you; when

the market's ability and inclination to pay the prices you need to command to sustain yourself decline; when people's tastes change; when other places where vacationers can spend their discretionary dollars out-think and out-invest and out-promote you; when you expand with money that costs more than your revenues can support; when you think you can suspend the immutable laws of economics; and when your hubris deludes you into believing you're as smart as your dog thinks you are....Any of these elements can lead to a downward spiral.

With the benefit of hindsight, and a few years of graduate study in the school of hard knocks, I think I'm on very firm ground when I reveal how you can make a small fortune in the ski business: start off with a large one.

Despite some ominous clouds, American Skiing continued to invest in major improvements in the Mountain during the final years of the decade. Warren Cook resigned in 1999, giving way to the John Diller era. I hope this book can, in some small way, pay sufficient tribute to Warren's contribution to Sugarloaf. He was, if there ever was one, the right man at the right time. He steadied a foundering ship, steered it through the worst of economic shoals, devoted every ounce of his energy and considerable talent to refocusing the Mountain on what had accounted for its initial success—its skiing—and demonstrated that a successful enterprise is, at its best, merely the lengthened shadow of its leader. He believed, and still believes, in Sugarloaf's greatness and potential. We all hope and truly believe that he will get a chance to see his belief vindicated.

The Town of Carrabassett Valley purchased the former Crockertown public lot for $424,000 in 2000, from the State of Maine. The Anti-Gravity Center was built for Carrabassett Valley Academy, and discussions began on a major improvement plan for the Narrow Gauge Pathway on the old railroad bed. This would be funded with a $600,000 grant, along with some additional town funds.

So the 1990s saw great change and great growth. Snowboarding,

*Everyone's favorite lift operator, Dennis Parsons (1948–2007).*

Telemark Skiing, and freestyle had changed for the better the old sport of alpine skiing. Shaped skis were beginning to revolutionize the way new skiers learned and old skiers skied. (I'll always remember a ride up the Quad with Tom "Coach" Reynolds in 1996, after we'd skied together for several hours. When I asked him

how I was skiing, he put his arm around me and said, "John, old boy, I've got good news and I've got bad news. The good news is, you're skiing just as well as you were the day you left here in 1968. The bad news is—we don't ski like that anymore. Get your feet apart!")

The only question on Sugarloafers' minds at the end of the twentieth century was: Who will ultimately own this place, and how will it affect us?

**Above:** *Chip Carey and Warren Cook.*
**Below:** *John Diller.*
**Right:** *Warren Cook*

**113**

# The Dream Abides:
## *2000–*

### 6

irst, a word or two about my chosen title for this final chapter in the Sugarloaf Story. Fans of the Coen Brothers' movies—and I count myself among the most rabid, even though I'm not much of a moviegoer (I just choose them well)—consider *The Big Lebowski* to be one of their best.

In this classic, the star-crossed hero, one Jeffrey Lebowski, is mistaken for another Lebowski from whom some scurrilous scoundrels are attempting to extract some serious money. The trials and tribulations that Jeffrey, who refers to himself as "The Dude," endures are hilarious, and in most cases brought upon himself by a combination of his naiveté, his substance-induced foggy state of mind, and the stupidity of his friends. After all is said and done, he survives to flounder along for another day. When asked how things are going, he responds, "The Dude abides."

Webster tells us one definition of the word abide is "to continue to endure," and that's how The Dude meant it. And that's how I mean it in the title of this chapter. The dream **does** endure. And the dream is one that includes the hopes of Amos and the Bigelow Boys, of Bunny Bass and George Cary and King Cummings and Warren Cook, and now multiple generations of Sugarloafers from Maine and afar who share a deep devotion to this special place.

Through prosperous and difficult times, through certainty and uncertainty, through blizzards and dry spells, the spirit of Sugarloaf has not only endured—it has flourished. I see it in the faces and I hear it in the whoops and hollers of little ones who are just discovering the sport, and skiers even older than I who've found an unbroken patch of new powder. (Note to Ski Patrol

nemesis Rick Chenard: Those ropes are there for a reason.)

There's something about the combination of our exhilarating sport, the unique terrain on the north side of a fairly remote mountain in Maine, and the camaraderie that I think only skiers are able to enjoy, that guarantees the dream **will** abide.

*"Crusher" Wilkinson*

As John Diller said in a letter to Sugarloafers in December 2000, kicking off Sugarloaf's fiftieth anniversary year:

*As I write this letter, I realize that, in fact, over the past 50 years, not much has changed. Yes, we have more trails, better lifts, and a road; but it's still about a mountain, a skier, and an inspiration. And we have Amos to thank for that.*

Back to the story. The 2000–01 season stands out for a couple of reasons. On the third day of the season, Paul Schipper skied his 3,240th day of "The Streak," and it would continue until January 3, 2005, when he would reach 3,903 days before illness would interfere with, but not stop, his skiing.

And Sugarloafers spent the winter celebrating fifty years of skiing on the mountain, with all events masterfully organized and executed by Jim Costello. John Diller was clearly the man in charge, and his teaching and coaching roots provided a great connection with the kind of skiers who made Sugarloaf their mountain of choice.

American Skiing (ASC) continued to invest in Sugarloaf's facilities, as well as its marketing efforts. Industry estimates put Sugarloaf's revenues for the 2000–01 season at about $10 million, and Sunday River's at three to four times that. Both mountains were apparently capable of operating in the black, but ASC's financial situation continued to be perilous as a result of many factors: its huge investment in other areas it owned, especially in the development of The Canyons in Utah; difficulty in divesting itself of some of its properties or selling some, like Sugarbush, at a discounted price; legal difficulties surrounding the aborted sale of Steamboat; lenders holding high-interest debt who demanded those loans be serviced; and the delisting of its stock due to its price falling below an acceptable threshold.

In March, despite an encouraging season—with an estimated 355,000 skier visits at Sugarloaf and 547,000 at Sunday River—corporate-wide problems resulted in the board's replacing Les Otten as chairman with an experienced resort professional, B. J. Fair. Otten maintained an office at Sunday River, and remained on the board for a time before going on to pursue other interests.

Skier visits in 2001–02 dropped to 331,000 at Sugarloaf and 520,000 at Sunday River, attributed mainly to uncooperative winter weather in general, especially on weekends.

In the fall of 2002, Diller was placed in charge of operations at both Sugarloaf and Sunday River, with his office at the latter. John's thirty-two years of experience would be tested, as the change in management structure combined the staffs at both areas and resulted in layoffs of some longtime employees. The continuing financial pressures caused the Corporation to reduce expenditures on maintenance and capital improvements.

As someone who skis some fifty days a year at Sugarloaf—with an occasional foray to another area for a little variety, to meet up with old friends, or to explore a new resort—I think I can attest that John Diller, "Crusher" Wilkinson, and the whole Sugarloaf crew have passed the test. The Sugarloaf experience, despite whatever might have been happening to the Corporation's finances in recent years, has continued to be first-class.

I will say that I don't envy John and his team, caught as they are in a tough business at a tough time, responding to leadership half a continent away, and trying to meet the demanding expectations of an increasingly discerning market that expects, for good reason, a superior skiing experience given the price they're asked to pay.

Very savvy marketing of season-pass products that combine ASC's New England ski areas in an affordable way has provided not only a welcome preseason infusion of cash, but also a guarantee of both a revenue stream and traffic on the Mountain to support other profit centers. Reduced ticket prices for Maine residents on Maine Days and similar promotions have generated traffic and revenue that might otherwise not have been realized. I learned a lesson from Walt Schoenknecht nearly forty years ago: A chairlift seat is a perishable product, and every time one goes up empty, the potential income has been lost forever. Since it costs the same to send the chair up full or empty, it pays to fill it at whatever price you can get.

On the Mountain, expansion and upgrades to the snowmaking

system, along with trail improvements and opening more off-piste terrain, have continued during recent years, and specialized facilities for snowboarders have been installed and continually upgraded.

The Sugarloaf Outdoor Center features more than 100 kilometers of well-groomed cross-country skiing, thanks to the activity of a bombardier groomer.

The golf course continues to attract golfers to its challenging, spectacularly beautiful track, and has proven to increase the attractiveness of the area for both conventioneers and retirees. A spectacular clubhouse, made possible by the overwhelming support of the residents of Carrabassett Valley, who approved its construction, has replaced the makeshift operation of twenty years in the lower terminal of the West Mountain Chair. The $1 million, 5,500-square-foot facility includes an expanded pro shop with a panoramic view of the Bigelow Mountain range. The dining room, lounge, and porch overlook the tenth and eleventh tees, with the Crocker Cirque in the background. The expansive dining room seats sixty guests inside and up to one hundred when the patio and porch are used. The clubhouse also features a telecommunications area, locker rooms, and a large practice putting green.

Real estate activity has not only not leveled off, but has actually accelerated in recent years. More and more property owners are spending time in the area outside of ski season, and any summer day will see kayakers, canoers, hikers, and bikers taking advantage of what the region has to offer.

Yes, it's a far cry from the idea of hacking out a trail for a few folks to ski to the resort of today.

Sugarloafers await what lies ahead as eagerly as they press their faces to the window in November to see the first flakes of snow.

And, indeed—the dream abides.

# Appendix A: *The People Who Got It Going*

*Note: This material was compiled by Dick Crommett shortly before his death, as part of his project to write a history of the town of Carrabassett Valley.*

### PEOPLE WHO CLEARED THE ACCESS ROAD AND CUT WINTER'S WAY:

Chester Atwood Jr.

Emerson Barrow

Vernon Dexter

Howard Dunham

Wendell Dunham

Roscoe "Mickey" Durrell

Roland Fotter

Kendric Lane

Taito Maki

Donald "Kid" Murray

Hayden Nichols

Russell Riggs

Russell Seavey

Robert "Stub" Taylor

Odlin Thompson

Austin Thompson Jr.

Glen Turner

Harry Vose

Edgar Vose Jr.

Amos Winter

### PEOPLE WHO WERE INVOLVED IN THE ESTABLISHMENT OF THE SUGARLOAF MOUNTAIN CORP.:

#### Officers:

Robert N. "Bunny" Bass, President

C. Richard Luce, Vice President

Richard H. Bell, Secretary and Clerk

James P. Flint, Treasurer

#### Directors:

Fletcher H. Brown

Benjamin Butler

George F. Cary II

Horace W. Chapman

William Kierstead

George Mendall

Herbert Preston

Allan Quimby

Robert T. Scott

Rand N. Stowell

William Vaughan

Amos G. Winter Jr.

Clarence Wyman

### Other people who helped in the early days:

George Albert

Harry Baxter

Harvey Boynton

Charles Clark

Eleanor Clark

John Clark

Peg Clark

Warren Cook

H. King Cummings

Karl "Dutch" Demshar

David Gurnsey

Sel Hannah

Bill Hatch

Robert Henderson

Jean Luce

Norton Luce

Wes Marco

Fred Morrison

Herbert Preston

Ed Rogers

Scott Scully

Phin Sprague

Leo Tague

Larry Warren

Martha Webber

Peter Webber

Bruce White

# Appendix B: *Sugarloafers in the Maine Ski Hall of Fame*

Karl Anderson

"Bunny" Bass

Dick Bell

Fletcher Brown

John Christie

Irv Kagan

Jean Luce

Jack Lufkin

Wes Marco

"Pat" Murphy

Roger Page

Tom Reynolds

"Stub" Taylor

Peter Webber

Amos G. Winter Jr.

# Appendix C: *Sugarloaf/USA Golf Club Ratings and Awards*

*Best of Northeast Golf:*   Best Overall Courses, 2006

*Boston Magazine:*   Top 10 Golf Holes in New England (11th Hole), 1996

*Fine Arts of Fairway:*   Cover, 11th Hole, 1999

*Golf Digest:*   #30 of America's Top 100 Greatest Public Courses, 2005

#1 Golf Course in Maine for 20 Consecutive Years, 2005

#45 of America's Top 100 Greatest Public Courses, 2003

Top 100 You Can Play in the USA, 1999

Top 10 Courses in the USA for Memorability and Aesthetics, 1997

#1 Upscale Course You Can Play in New England, 1996

#23 of the Top 75 Upscale Courses You Can Play in the USA, 1996

*Golf for Women*   #16 of the Best Places to Play in America, 1998

*Golf Magazine:*   Top 100 Courses You Can Play, 2004, 2002, 2000

#1 Course You Can Play in New England, 1998

#20 of the Top 100 You Can Play in the USA, 1998 New England, 2005

*Golfweek:*   #41 of America's Best 100 Golf Resorts, 2005

#1 Public Course in Maine, 2003

#1 Public Course in Maine, 2002

#1 Golf Course in Maine, 1997

*Links Magazine:*   #14 of the Hidden Gems that Anyone Can Play, 2000

*Men's Journal:*   Best Golf Course in the Northeast, 1996

Best Mountain Course in the USA, 1996

*NE Journal of Golf*   #1 of the Top 100 Courses You Can Play in New England, 2002–2004

*Ski Magazine:*   Top 30 Summer Resorts in USA, 2001

Cover Photo of the 11th Hole in 1998

Top 12 Mountain Golf Courses in North America, 1997

*Sports Illustrated:*   Hole #14 the Featured Hole in Golf Calendar, 2000

# Appendix D: *Sugarloafer Mountain Ski-Club Presidents*

Horace Chapman (1950–52)

Robert Bass (1952–54)

Scott Scully (1954–56)

Bill Kierstead (1956–57)

Jay Winter (1957–58)

Harvey Boynton (1958–59)

Leo Tague (1959–61)

Burt Covert (1961–62)

Don Pfeifle (1962–64)

Charlie Clark (1964–65)

John Christie (1965–66)

Norton Luce (1966–68)

Skip Skaling (1968–70)

Peter Spalding (1970–72)

Jack Smart (1972–73)

Bernie Carpenter (1973–75)

Bob Waddle (1975–77)

Charlie Murray (1977–79)

Frank Woodard (1979–80)

Pat Andrews (1980–82)

Tina Hinckley (1982–83)

Jon Hellstedt (1983–90)

John Lacasse (1990–93)

Marvin Collins (1993–95)

Greg Foster (1995–99)

Sue Manter (1999–2001)

Charlotte Zahn (2001–03)

Lev Steeves (2003–04)

Bruce Miles (2004–  )